New Product Programs

NEW PRODUCT PROGRAMS

Their Planning and Control

David B. Uman

American Management Association, Inc.

Standard Book Number: 8144-5181-0

Library of Congress catalog card number: 72-78604

First printing

To
My Wife
Susan
and My Two Sons
Michael and Jonathan

Preface

BY 1968 it had become obvious that classical management techniques were unable to solve the planning and control problems related to product development programs. A new system was required, one that was specifically designed to handle the unique requirements of new product development programs.

During the past decade, the marketing concept gained rapid acceptance and placed unusually heavy demands on other more traditional functional organizational units, such as manufacturing and engineering. Rapid change to meet the demands of the marketplace required much greater flexibility and more intensive coordination between functional organizations. Out of these unique requirements came the product development planning and control system (PDPCS), a system that is concerned with the problems of planning and control in the dimensions of cost, schedule, performance, and information. The basic approach of this system is founded upon the technique of networking.

This integrated management system is applicable to any product development activity in any industry. Although the technique has been tested mainly in the consumer products and retail management fields, there is no reason why it cannot be successful in any product development application.

This system was initially developed, refined, and thoroughly tested at Lever Brothers Company, New York, one of the nation's largest manufacturers and marketers of consumer-oriented products in the United States. Developed first on an experimental basis, the system was expanded across all divisions of the company. Now, all new product development activity approved for test marketing and national launch is in some phase of the total system. The principles and procedures illustrated in this book have been refined and proved in repeated successful applications over the course of a number of years. They are highly effective for planning, evaluating, and controlling other new product development programs, no matter how large or complex.

The most important lesson to be learned from the study and implementation of this system is the need to define the objectives and work to be accomplished in each new product program in terms of the various elements and interdependencies involved. Instead of a vast, uncontrollable complex program, one thus is able to undertake in planned succession the implementation of a series of discrete, recognizable tasks. By means of this process, it is possible to direct undiluted energy and attention toward the completion of each new product launch in a considered and deliberate manner. The clear definition of the work that must be done, the prompt recognition of potential deviations from the plan, and the feedback of information concerning schedule and cost are basic to success in the management and control of any project.

I wish to express my appreciation to Lever Brothers Company and its management for allowing me to develop the PDPCS and for sponsoring the preparation of this study. In particular, I would like to mention Monroe Kaufman, who offered continual guidance and a great many cogent, helpful, and encouraging suggestions. I also would like to thank Mrs. Bernadette Duffy, who typed the manuscript through all its revisions in the trying circumstances of a corporate headquarters office. Finally, it seems appropriate to acknowledge the support of my family, who accepted with forbearance the many weekends and holidays consumed in the preparation of this study.

DAVID B. UMAN

Contents

New Product Programs

Introduction

MANAGEMENT EXECUTIVES believe that a company's ability to remain competitive and to attain desired rates of growth depends in large part on its new product program. However, those product development control systems which utilize the techniques of early scientific management have been marked by a notable lack of success. This is evidenced by the tremendously high failure rate of the new products introduced into the marketplace every year.

THE PLANNING PROBLEM

New product development programs are beset with problems whose impact is felt strongly throughout management. The factors responsible for the current failure of earlier management systems, the high failure rate of new product introductions, and the underlying intricate management problems of these programs are these:

1. Market requirements demand new products more frequently.
2. Product life is shorter than ever.
3. Technology is more complicated; hence development work and the construction of capital equipment take longer.
4. Investment in research and facilities must be recovered more rapidly through higher profit margins.

5. High risk, high cost, and a great possibility of failure are factors in all new product development programs.
6. There is a high probability of cost increases and time slippages against original estimates.
7. Complex relationships and interdependencies lead to great difficulty in coordinating diverse operating organizations.
8. Unique techniques, timetables, and decisions of diverse operating organizations present problems in new product development.
9. It is difficult to estimate time and costs for progress with a high degree of technical accuracy.
10. Lack of clear-cut technical and priority objectives results in a high degree of change in program direction.
11. Introductory marketing campaigns are often poorly planned or inadequate.

An additional characteristic of research and development programs must be emphasized—the high degree of uncertainty involved. Along with this, there is usually also the larger problem of scarcity of resources (qualified personnel to carry out the work) for R&D programs.

Once specific objectives are established, new product development programs have certain planning and control requirements. These include:

- The need to identify all the activities required to meet the objectives.
- The need to pinpoint complex interrelationships or constraints among these activities, including organizational and technical interfaces.
- The need to predict with a reasonable degree of certainty the time and cost of all these activities.
- The need to "optimize" or allocate limited resources in the best possible manner among activities.
- The need for flexibility—that is, for the ability to update the program under conditions of change.
- The need to control the execution of the program.
- The need to identify tradeoffs between cost, lead time, marketability, capital, risk, and other factors.

There are two major categories of product development programs. Some programs require the combination of many diverse elements, all generally based on a known technology, to meet an end objective. Examples are product changeovers (new models) and sales promotions. Programs which require extensive research and development to reach such goals as new products belong to the second category. The most common characteristic of these programs is their special-purpose nature, even though in both categories there may be found some individual elements with a conventional production-volume and market-supply character.

SIGNIFICANCE OF ORGANIZED PLANNING

Certain advantages accrue to the firm that is first into the market with a newly developed product having a high market appeal. In the first place, the product enjoys a privileged position in the marketplace. Rival products, later marketed by competitors, must be accompanied by considerable investment and expense—that is, marketing power— to cut into the market domination enjoyed by the initiating firm. When the delay is exceptionally long, the new entrant may be faced with little opportunity for profit. In the light of this, there may be a strong temptation to rush a product into the market without sufficient market investigation or testing. The substantial risks of pursuing either extreme are obvious.

There are several reasons why the job of coordinating new product activities is so difficult. First, the process of moving a product from the laboratory to the marketplace is divided into a number of stages: the generating and screening of ideas, preliminary market appraisal, technical development, marketing, sales and promotional planning, market testing, production, and initial distribution—each of which involves its own unique set of techniques, timetables, and decisions.

Second, a new product venture puts the entire company to the test. Each stage—from idea conception to eventual market launching— calls for a high degree of teamwork on the part of such diverse organizational units as research, manufacturing, marketing, sales, purchasing, and packaging. Coordinating the efforts of these units poses serious difficulties in the management of new product projects.

Certain interfaces exist between operating units which cause constraints at the start of specific activities. Communication lines must be established and maintained between all these elements. Of even greater importance is tying them together so that the desired goal, the successful launching of the product, will be reached according to plan.

Today's requirements for planning and control of product development programs can be met by the management techniques developed within the past decade. During that time, weapons-system-oriented industries with complex special-purpose programs have utilized management science techniques to cope with the time, cost, and performance requirements unique to those programs. Out of these efforts came the management tools now commonly associated with the defense industry. These tools include many of the concepts of operations research and systems engineering as well as PERT, CPM, line of balance, program management, configuration management, learning curve techniques, value engineering, and cost effectiveness.

Recently, these management techniques have been utilized in non-weapons-system industries. Commercial businesses, normally five to ten years behind the defense industries, are discovering that modern management techniques not only have direct application to their problems, but can be instrumental in solving the problems as well.

New product planning and development programs have many characteristics in common with defense-system programs. This fact explains the failure of earlier management systems and the need to turn to modern systems techniques in order to develop a planning and control system specifically designed for product development programs. The tangible and intangible benefits to be achieved with an effective planning and control system are as follows:

1. A basic improvement in product development planning which allows for better decision making prior to entering upon new product programs.
2. A greatly improved ability to control new product programs against original objectives and within the original estimates of time and cost.
3. A better evaluation of the effects of uncertainty and risk in new product programs.
4. The possibility of executing a new product program with an optimal use of resources such as manpower and money.
5. The potential for actual cost savings, increases in organizational efficiency, and improvement in profits.

6. Effective communication among persons working toward a common goal.
7. The opportunity for trade-offs among time, cost, and performance criteria.

OTHER INFORMATION ON NEW PRODUCT PLANNING AND CONTROL

There is ample literature available on new product planning, organization for new product development, product development activities, and marketing of new products. The major sources of this information are industry and management associations and management consultant organizations, most notably the American Management Association, the National Industrial Conference Board, and Booz, Allen & Hamilton Inc. Both AMA and NICB have published books on new product development based on the experience of major executives of large corporations engaged in new product programs. Booz, Allen & Hamilton is a management consulting firm which has published material relevant to new product development problems.

The major inadequacy of any literature on product development programs as they relate to planning and control systems is that investigation has been sparse in this area and little pertinent information is available. The existing literature concentrates on top management appraisals of development programs with strategic overviews of their impact; organizational aspects of new product development; research and development considerations in terms of work flow, evaluation of projects and commercialization of research results, reasons for failure of marketing programs; new product planning; problems of coordination (with few recommendations for improvement); and the complexity of new product programs.

There is also much information available on the new management tools of planning and control. The major sources of this information are the U.S. Government, defense industry firms, management associations, data processing manufacturers, and a few books. The Federal Government, in particular, has published many volumes on PERT/time, PERT/cost, and line of balance. These publications are largely technique-oriented; they concentrate mainly on the specifics of the technique, not on application. The Federal Government requires that these techniques be utilized as part of its contracts. In any literature which discusses application, the main emphasis is on the defense systems manufacturer.

Since 1964 several magazine articles have appeared which have described the application of network analysis techniques to individual new product planning and development programs. Though these articles reveal how the technique was used on specific programs on a one-time basis, no consideration is given to extensions and the development of a total product planning system.

This book goes beyond these single-application studies of network analysis techniques; it proposes an integrated management planning and control system that satisfies the requirements of high-risk, one-time, new product development programs and the organizational considerations required for these programs. This study shows how the application of a whole gamut of modern management planning and control techniques, when properly implemented and organized, can help reduce the risk, lead time, and cost while at the same time reducing the failure rate of new product programs.

LIMITATIONS

An integrated planning and control system implies the rapid processing of information for analysis and control. For a large-scale project, the most rapid means of processing project information is through a computer. Computer systems to handle this task are readily available from almost every major EDP manufacturer. The details of computer programs are not discussed in these pages. However, suggestions are made in this area should there be further interest. It should *not* be assumed that computer use or access is mandatory for the success of the integrated planning and control system. Manual means of processing information are possible and, in the case of small programs, sometimes desirable. However, as the planning system is presented here, information processing and output reports are computer-oriented. Should computer access not be available, adaptations will be necessary.

The details of new product planning and development programs are also omitted. For example, the problems of marketing, research and development, engineering, and other departments in development programs as applied to these specialties are not our concern. The main emphasis is on systems and techniques of planning and controlling product development programs.

For the most part, the planning concepts developed here apply *after* a decision is made to develop a specific product idea. This point is generally reached when top management approves the initiation of development work by a marketing or development team on a unique product or service idea that can be clearly defined within specific overall objectives. Preparatory steps—approaches to generating product ideas, methods of selecting commercially feasible product ideas from those generated, techniques for screening those selected in order to meet company profit, return on investment, and other goals—are not analyzed, although there is no doubt a great need to develop approaches to these important steps. Modern techniques are available, but they need to be integrated into an overall structural framework that is readily usable by businessmen.

Within this book are a number of concepts and techniques that apply to the generalized planning and control problem as presented. These concepts are defined briefly and then developed into an overall structural framework for planning and control.

The following concepts are used throughout the book:

Program management. This is a general management activity encompassing planning, control, supervision, and the engineering or manufacturing involved in producing an end item. It is similar to functional management and administration in that it is basically getting work done through people, with all that this implies in regard to objectives, incentives, and communication. It requires the program manager to have very specific objectives which, when achieved, mean the end of his function. It implies no line authority over the organizations that produce the items.

Project definition. This involves the refinement of specifications and the detailing of time and cost estimates in order to reduce to a minimum the uncertainties in a program. These uncertainties include primary mission goals, major performance goals, scope, restrictions, ground rules, decision points, methods, and decision rules.

Work breakdown structure. This is a family-tree subdivision of a program from which time and cost are planned and controlled. It defines the major areas of work effort and their relationships, beginning with end objectives, and establishes a common framework for structuring of networks.

Decision tree methodology. Decision tree methodology results from explicit recognition of future alternatives, possible outcomes, and decisions which can result from an initial or "present" decision under question. The name decision tree stems from the graphical portrayal, which allows branches for each possible alternative for a given decision and branches for each possible outcome (event) which can result from each alternative.

Risk analysis. Risk analysis is the identification of alternatives and consequences to be made with the detailed analysis of individual consequence chains under conditions of certainty, risk, or uncertainty. An evaluation scheme is necessary to reveal the preferred consequence chain stemming from an alternative. A choice is made in favor of the alternative with the most attractive consequence.

The primary purpose of this book is to improve the planning and control of those business programs common to non-weapons industries. With this end in view, it presents a planning and control system particularly applicable to product development programs. However, the overall approach and the specific techniques are of value in any one-time-through, high-risk programs that require close coordination of interrelated complex technologies or specialized functions.

The first section describes the need for planning and control in product development programs. This need is extended to the relationship of these management concepts to product development programs. Then network analysis and project management concepts in general are discussed. Finally, an integrated planning and control system is proposed that satisfies the unique requirements of product development programs.

However, in developing a planning and control system, additional questions must be answered in order to integrate the system into a useful conceptual framework. These questions include the following:

- What kind of organization is required to implement a planning and control system for new product development?
- How is such a system integrated into the present organization?
- How should the planning of product development programs be structured?

- What planning techniques can be used for new product programs?
- How do you determine who does what?
- What are the means for describing program objectives?
- What kind of information is made available to top management for decision making?
- What information does top management need for releasing capital to highly uncertain development programs?
- What are the major system outputs? How are these outputs presented, interpreted, and used?
- What kind of system controls are required to define responsibility for each major output? Update program status? Report program schedule and cost to top management? Communicate program status to diverse organizational units?
- What kind of system extensions can be used to apply company resources where needed? Resolve time slippages and cost overruns? Maintain product quality and reliability?

Implicit in developing these planning and control concepts is the assumption that the reader has some knowledge of network analysis techniques. Although network analysis is described, a full treatment is not included; suffice it to say that in the years since it was developed in 1957 it has become a recognized contemporary management technique.

On the other hand, project management techniques, as developed in the defense industries through the impetus of the Department of Defense, are relatively unknown in commercial industry. For this reason, no prior knowledge of this concept is assumed. In addition, project management concepts are developed as an important planning and control system extension.

This book is divided into three parts. The first part (Chapters 1 and 2) provides a background for product development planning and reveals the requirements for planning and control of such programs.

Chapter 1 provides the background information of the product development planning and control problem. It discusses the importance of product development in American industry and the failure of classic management techniques to solve planning and control problems related to product development programs. This is done within the framework of the evolution of planning and control techniques as developed for production-oriented, engineering-oriented, and marketing-oriented organizations. From this, an investigation of planning and control requirements of development programs to set the objectives of a system is considered.

Chapter 2 discusses the nature of product development programs, including typical program stages and time spans for introduction of new products. Planning requirements of new product development programs are then explored, including the prerequisites of good planning, time/cost/performance factors, setting objectives, scheduling, resource allocation, and program constraints. Control requirements of new product development planning are also dealt with, including progress reporting and budgeting.

The second part (Chapter 3) focuses on two major and specific concepts, network analysis and program management, presented here as the organizational and conceptual framework of an overall product planning system.

As a preface to the system description, Chapter 3 briefly describes network analysis methodology—definitions, network logic, time estimating, network calculations, and critical path concepts. Program management concepts are explored as an organizational framework for planning and control. A description of program management concepts is given, and the impact of these concepts on present organizational structures is explained. This sets the framework for the application of program management concepts to commercial organizations for development programs.

The last part (Chapters 4, 5, and 6) develops an integrated planning and control system specifically designed for new product programs.

The major aspects of a product development planning and control system are described in Chapter 4 in the sequence in which the system operates. Because of its feedback characteristics, the system is represented as a cycle with two components: the planning cycle and the control cycle. The planning cycle (Chapter 5) includes organization and system training, project definition, work breakdown structures and decision tree methodology, and the details of networking, preparing schedules, and replanning. The control cycle (Chapter 6) includes plan approval, updating the plan, output reports, project evaluation and management action involving extensions (simulation, risk analysis, and so on), and higher management reports. In addition, the details of management and execution of the program are also included.

I

The Need for Effective Planning and Control of Product Development Programs

IN A RECENT STUDY by the National Industrial Conference Board on the future of marketing, the major findings indicated that although the marketing concept offered great opportunities for corporate success, it frequently encountered serious obstacles to progress.[1] One of the five major marketing challenges most frequently cited was new product development.

The Importance of Product Development

Much of the impetus for new product innovation stems from three interrelated needs: (1) the need to match the new product

[1] The Conference Board, *The Marketing Executive Looks Ahead*, Experiences in Marketing Management No. 13 (New York: National Industrial Conference Board, 1967), ⌐ 1.

entries marketed by competitors; (2) the need to cope with changing customers' changing requirements and preferences; and (3) the need to keep pace with accelerated gains in technology.[2] But, if the successful development of new products and services answers these needs, carrying out such programs and developing the capability to live with rapid change are the major steps to be taken.

Definition and Objectives of Product Development

In general, product development involves product research, product improvement, and product development activities; it involves a company's efforts to insure future products that will yield a maximum return on stockholders' investments, whether by addition of new products to old lines, improvement of old products, or addition of new product lines. Its various aspects are further defined as follows:

Product development. Proven principles are applied to developing a working model to determine the components necessary to meet a predetermined set of specifications.

Industrial research. New principles and combinations of known elements are sought with a specific commercial objective in mind.

Product engineering. Materials, components, and methods of construction are decided upon which result in the most economical commercial product producible with the existing facilities or facilities which can be readily and economically obtained.

Product planning. Development time, engineering, facilities, manufacturing, tooling, money, and capital investment facilities are committed to those products which have a customer acceptance low enough to produce volume sales at a profitable price. The search, screening, development, and commercialization of new products are marked out and supervised; existing lines are modified; and marginal and unprofitable items are discontinued.

A product has two key characteristics: (1) *technology*, the fund of knowledge, technical and otherwise, which enables economic production of the product, and (2) *markets*, to whom and how the product is to be sold, which enable profitable distribution. These two

[2] *Ibid.*, p. 37.

EXHIBIT I.   TWO-DIMENSIONAL CHARACTERISTICS OF PRODUCTS

———————————— Increased Technical Newness ————————————▶

Product objectives	No technological change	Improved technology	New technology
No market change		Reformulation	Replacement
Strengthened market	Remerchandizing	Improved product	Product line extension
New market	New use	Market extension	Diversification

Increasing Market Requirements (label along left vertical axis, with downward arrow)

Source: Based on Samuel C. Johnson and Conrad Jones, "How to Organize for New Products," *Harvard Business Review* (May-June 1957), p. 52.

characteristics are inseparable, because an invention is not a new product until it is produced and distributed in a form that people can and will buy.

As shown in Exhibit 1, there are varying degrees of product newness in each of two dimensions. In the technological dimension, the requirements for new technical knowledge, machinery, or plant may range from none to an entirely new spectrum of technical and production knowledge. The marketing requirements also range from no change in customers, sales, or channels of distribution to a need for developing both new customers and new distribution channels. Numerous variations in the degree of newness lie along both dimensions of this grid.

In general, the objectives of product development are to sell more goods and to realize greater profits. Specifically, the objectives of product development are [3]

[3] The Conference Board, *New Product Development: I. Selection—Coordination—Financing*, Studies in Business Policy No. 40 (New York: National Industrial Conference Board, 1950), p. 11.

1. To arouse customer interest and stimulate sales so as to hold or increase the company's share of existing markets.
2. To utilize idle production and sales facilities by opening new markets.
3. To keep the company's products and product lines in a strong competitive position.
4. To diversify product lines so as to reduce seasonal and long-term fluctuations in production and sales.
5. To replace products which, because of market saturation or intensified competition, have declining profits.

As can be seen, product development programs are mainly due to marketing implications—which can be either external or internal to a company's operations. External implications are environmental conditions that allow a company to engage in product development. These include increasing customer incomes, changes in the nature of population distribution that open new markets, increasing percentage of the aged, changes in industrial markets and buyers' needs, and research which leads to new products that can satisfy latent needs.

Internal implications involve the problem of excess capacity, including excessive production and financial capacity as well as excessive marketing facilities. These categories of excess capacity may be the result of (1) changes in demand, (2) instability of competitive positions in an oligopoly market, and (3) prosperity. Internal factors also include cyclical and seasonal shifts in capacity.

CAUSES OF PRODUCT DEVELOPMENT FAILURE

In 1957, A. C. Nielsen, Jr., graphically pointed out the rigorous challenge of product development activity. He found that, over the ten previous years, three out of every five leading brands had been knocked out of first place. In an analysis of these failures, Nielsen found that 77 percent of the products lost out because of shortcomings in product development work.

Recent findings indicate that the problem is still just as acute. Present-day marketing managers are discovering that three out of every ten major products now being marketed fail in some important respect to come up to expectations. In addition, one of the three is considered so disappointing that it is withdrawn completely from the market.

Some of the reasons for the high failure rate are

1. Lack of a well-thought-out marketing plan.
2. Introduction of products before they have been adequately tested under conditions of actual use.
3. Inaccurate appraisals of the need for a product, the extent of its market, and the competition it will face from similar or substitute products.
4. Insufficient product research.
5. A poorly planned or inadequate introductory marketing campaign.
6. Lack of pretesting of the package.
7. Higher costs than anticipated.
8. Inadequate sales force.
9. Product defects.
10. Poor timing.
11. Weakness in distribution.[4]

The most common obstacles to the introduction of a new product are impatience, insufficient planning and preparation, lack of understanding of the market for the product, and lack of the necessary time, labor, and money to put it over.

Today, when so many new products are pouring forth from industry, and the competition for the attention of buyers is so great, it cannot be assumed a product will sell simply because it is good. A company seeking national distribution must plan and work for it. In some areas, such as the packaged goods field, competition is so intense that an advertising and promotion tour de force is required to obtain sufficient consumer acceptance to induce retailers to put the product on their shelves. And the cost of such a campaign is so great that the process is called "buying into the market." Because of the cost and effort generally involved in launching new products, many products suffer a prolonged period of profitless sales before they pro-

---

[4] The Conference Board, *New Product Development: III. Marketing New Products*, Studies in Business Policy No. 69 (New York: National Industrial Conference Board, 1954), p. 7; and "Why New Products Fail," *The Conference Board Record*, October 1964, pp. 11–18.

EXHIBIT 2.   NONMANUFACTURING COSTS INVOLVED IN THE
DEVELOPMENT AND DISTRIBUTION OF
PRODUCTS THAT FAIL

DIRECT COSTS

1. Engineering.

2. Tooling.

3. Package design.

4. Advertising.

5. Merchandising.

6. Direct selling.

7. Administration.

8. Warehousing.

9. Inventory.

10. Price concessions.

11. Extra advertising allowances to distributors and dealers.

12. Goodwill adjustments.

13. Unfavorable factory variances (resulting from necessary reduction in production schedules).

INDIRECT COSTS

1. Lower morale.

2. Lost prestige.

3. Damaged trade relations.

4. Valuable time and effort taken from other products.

5. Loss of advertising and promotion money needed for profitable projects.

Source: Robert M. Oliver, "The Marketing Concept in Developing Products for Profit," *Developing a Product Strategy,* AMA Management Report 39, 1959, p. 73.

duce income for the originating company. (See Exhibit 2 for non-manufacturing costs involved in development and distribution of products that fail.) But a poor marketing plan may not only defer the realization of profit on a new product; it may impair the profit potential or eliminate all hope of profit. Delay in achieving a market position may give more aggressive competitors an opportunity to meet the challenge and, in such fast-moving fields as chemicals, may permit them to take over the market.

COMPLEXITY OF PRODUCT DEVELOPMENT

The impact of a product development project is felt throughout a company. Research and development, engineering, production, and marketing departments share major responsibility for developing and introducing a product. In the course of development, all departments —finance, market research, legal, advertising, and the rest—either take an active part in the work or are called on for advice and opinions. Because of the complexity of such projects, cooperation among departments at various steps in the development process is of the utmost importance. Lack of proper coordination lengthens the time required for development, increases the cost, and creates a chaotic situation within the organization. A well-coordinated program, on the other hand, permits the work to flow smoothly with a minimum of lost time and interdepartmental friction.

Research and development organizations in particular have unique problems in product development programs. Chief among these problems are establishing development schedules and coordinating the transition to production. Research and development problems center around

1. The need to keep R&D men free of trouble-shooting jobs so they can devote a maximum amount of time to development work.
2. The need for an adequate forecast of time requirements that takes into consideration the changing nature of individual projects and the varying amounts of time required to get completed projects into production.
3. The need to place a limit on the quantity of projects undertaken

EXHIBIT 3.   EVOLUTION OF A PRODUCT FROM RESEARCH

	RESEARCH CENTER					DIVISION	
	RESEARCH		ENGINEERING		COMMERCIALIZATION		
	Basic Research	Exploratory Research	Product Development	Technical Market Analysis	Design for Production	Tooling	Production

........Applied research........   ....Product improvement........Application........Sales........

Engineering   Engineering   Engineering

Nonproduct oriented   Product oriented

Corporate supported   Division supported

Research center interests and obligations

Division interests and obligations

Overlapping functions requiring coordination, liaison, and assignment based on specific circumstances

Per: Robert S. Ingersoll
President
Borg-Warner Corporation

in order to avoid the dissipation of effort that results from overloading research personnel.

4. The constant changing of priorities on individual research projects.
5. The interruptions of projects resulting from personnel turnover.
6. The need to keep long-term projects active while adequately handling short-term projects.

Research and development organizations also have major problems in coordinating the transition to full-scale production. R&D responsibilities involve various aspects of packaging, product design, product testing, pilot plant runs, and patent protection. The coordination problems are a function of the product and its design as well as the difficulty of planning precisely, forecasting the production problems, and training production personnel. Manufacturing and production problems which R&D organizations must anticipate in making the transition from pilot plant operation to full-scale production include the following:

1. Lack of consistent quality and uniformity of components and raw materials purchased from different suppliers.
2. Raw materials defects requiring changes.
3. An increase in the large-scale handling of raw materials.
4. Startup and debugging of new equipment used in production lines.
5. Difficulties in determining quickly enough what new equipment is needed.
6. Difficulties in determining production rates and manufacturing standards.
7. Difficulties in establishing quality control limits, especially for raw materials and components.

Exhibit 3 shows the evolution of a product from research through commercialization. As the product emerges from exploratory research through product development, many functions overlap and require coordination, liaison, and assignment, the responsibilities for which rest with both research and operating division personnel.

Marketing executives feel that pressure for innovation is compounded as a result of the more rapid product obsolescence resulting from technological change. Many currently successful products are replacements for other ideas that have become obsolete because of changing technology. Developing the capability to live with rapid change is one of the bigger problems facing marketing organizations. This change manifests itself in these ways:

1. Market needs demand new products more frequently.
2. Product life is shorter.
3. Technology is more complicated; hence, development work and building of capital equipment take longer.
4. Investment in research and facilities must be recovered more rapidly through higher profit margins.[5]

ORGANIZATION FOR PRODUCT DEVELOPMENT

Within the corporate product development mainstream, three factors tend to complicate the establishment of cut-and-dried methods for accomplishing the necessary coordination:

1. A gradual shift of responsibility occurs as the project progresses from the laboratory through engineering, production, and sales. At each step, what has been done in previous steps must be considered, and information gained in the earlier work must be transferred along with the responsibility for carrying the project forward.
2. Not all projects follow the same pattern of development.
3. Any system of coordination must take into consideration the sensibilities of the individuals concerned.

Generally, a new product development program is divided into two separate activities: management and execution. *Management of the project* is concerned with (1) its preparation, its general supervision, and the acquisition of top management approval of changes; (2) the coordination of action required to execute the project; and (3) reporting, which may include requests for changes in schedules and additional appropriations for unforeseen contingencies. *The execution of the project* is handled by the appropriate departments, such as marketing, sales, manufacturing, or research and development.

[5] The Conference Board, *The Marketing Executive Looks Ahead, op. cit.*, p. 37.

The new product project manager leaves technical decisions to the department heads. Decisions on budgets and schedule deviations are referred to the next higher level of management for action.

In searching for ways to insure effective coordination of the various components of its new product program, a company needs to find the organizational approach most appropriate for its particular situation. Since there are several ways of providing organizationally for the coordination of new products, it is desirable to examine some of the factors that influence new product organization and that often determine the suitability of a particular approach for a given company.

A marketing coordinator at Monsanto Company has proposed the following two questions to separate "good" from "bad" new product organizational structures:

> (1) Is it crystal clear as to who or what group defines market needs initially and repeatedly? (2) Is that man or group so positioned in the organization as to be able to perform effectively and objectively—that is, is he or it really free to innovate, to put the company into new businesses, to marshal scattered resources, to implement recommendations? In other words, is the man or the group able to do all the things that must be done to introduce a new product?[6]

One of the factors that influence new product organization is the variety of new products. The job of coordination involved in a minor revision of a product in an existing line is often quite different from that required for developing a truly new product. Organizational problems differ with four basic new product classifications:

Type 1—a new model. Essentially an improvement on a current product in one or several of its characteristics, it is generally sold to the same customers for the same end uses as the current one.

Type 2—a new product in a familiar market. Essentially a new product, it has uses similar to those of present products and is sold in present markets or markets familiar to the company.

[6] The Conference Board, *Organizing for New Product Development*, Experiences in Marketing Management No. 11 (New York: National Industrial Conference Board, 1966), p. 16.

Type 3—a product new to the company, but not new to its markets. Essentially a new product to a company, it is sold in markets that are not new to competitors.

Type 4—a really new product introduced to a really new market. This is the kind of glamorous pioneering that, when it succeeds, makes headlines. When it fails, it is the butt of jokes in the company cloakrooms.

These categories and the variations shown in Exhibit 1 illustrate how one type of product development may require a completely different organizational approach from that required by another type.

A second factor which can affect the location and organizational arrangement for new product coordination is the orientation of the company. Because of the nature of their products, some companies have a primary interest in the technical or engineering considerations of their new product programs. As a result, they may tend to place great emphasis on linking new product direction closely to either their research and development units or their engineering units. Other companies feel that, although technical and engineering functions obviously have an important part to play in product development, a marketing orientation is even more essential for a new product program.

For the functionally organized company in which few, if any, activities are decentralized, the only question may be whether new product coordination is to be lodged within one major function, such as marketing, or given separate status. In the multidivision company, however, the situation is usually more complicated. It must be decided whether new product development and planning is to take place entirely at the division or corporate level or is to be carried out at both levels. The possibilities range from completely decentralized (divisional) responsibility to the centralization of all new product development at one point.

A third factor is placement of the responsibility. Primary responsibility for directing the new product effort can be vested in one individual, or it can be shared by several executives or units—or a division—within the company.

Effective organization for the new product function is essential. First, it provides top management with a means for controlling a vital part of the campaign's total effort. Second, it provides for the specific assignment of responsibility for getting an important job done. Third, it provides the vehicle through which people from many departments can work together to make the new product program a success.

A 1966 study of new product development organization by the National Industrial Conference Board identified seven different organization forms:

1. Product manager responsible for new products.
2. New product department responsible for new products as a staff department of the marketing organization.
3. New product department responsible for new products as staff of some department *other than* marketing.
4. New product department as staff to top-echelon management.
5. Separate department responsible for new products.
6. New product committees, composed of functional department heads.
7. New product task forces.[7]

Some of these organizational forms will be discussed after we have reviewed the classical management concepts which have failed to solve planning and control problems related to product development.

FAILURE OF CLASSICAL MANAGEMENT CONCEPTS

In discussing the failure of classical management concepts to solve planning and control problems related to product development programs, we shall explore the evolution of planning and control techniques from their early manifestations during the first decade of the twentieth century to the sophisticated techniques that have arisen from present and future programs. The needs and characteristics of these program types will be developed to include the classical techniques that are used to satisfy the needs and the reasons for failure of these techniques.

[7] *Ibid.*, pp. 28 31.

The Evolution of Planning and Control Techniques

Planning and control techniques were evolved from the foundations of scientific management theory established during the early 1900's by Frederick W. Taylor and his followers. Applied to the manufacturing segment of a business, scientific management principles found wide acceptance in American industry. As American industry expanded and national growth led to greater demand for products, more complex technology was required to produce goods. Planning and control emphasis then shifted to the engineering segment of a business. World War II forced an acceleration in the state of the art in engineering programs and created planning and control characteristics quite different from production-oriented systems. Further national growth led to the development of the marketing concept, a management approach which again shifted the emphasis of product planning and control to broader horizons—a total company outlook in organizing development programs.

It is ironic that, over a period of time, the development and application of planning and control techniques evolved from the specific requirements of production to the overall views of the marketing concept as applied to product development programs. This evolution is in inverse proportion to the development and application of other business techniques. Because of the complexity of new product development programs, this evolution is easy to trace.

Most planning techniques started in the business area where the planning variables were most easily quantified: production. At first, production planning and control systems were devised to satisfy high-volume production situations. As technology imposed time and cost constraints on production systems, planning and control techniques grew more sophisticated in order to resolve the resultant problems. Finally, the necessity to plan and control the product development programs which considered the requirements of diverse organizational units revealed that no classical technique had the unique operating characteristics of these programs. Therefore, unsuccessful attempts were made to adapt production-oriented and engineering-oriented techniques to the special requirements of new product development programs.

Basically, the planning and control needs of production created the next generation of techniques utilized by engineering-oriented organizations, such as line of balance. The specific needs of engineering led to a further sophistication of techniques. This development of second- and third-generation planning and control techniques, however, did not extend to marketing. This was because marketing's function is to determine the needs of consumers, which are extremely difficult (if not impossible) to specify. Production planning is based on clearly specified variables; engineering programs are less clear since technical specifications must be developed. Marketing program planning, on the other hand, is based on the criterion of consumer acceptance which must be estimated and is rarely specific or clear.

Because of the high degree of uncertainty of customer acceptance, marketing programs are high-risk programs: There exists the possibility of not reaching the objectives on time and within the limits of acceptable cost. This uncertainty in marketing programs requires a greater quantity of trade-offs between time, cost, and risks. Trade-offs can be considered the essence of management; and the need for more of them explains why marketing programs must be integrative with interfaces across diverse organizational units in order to obtain proper program performance.

We now have the framework for a new product development planning structure as it cuts across an organization. First, the marketing concept, operating at the highest level, requires that the needs of customers be probed in order to develop a product concept. A marketing organization, through market research or other techniques, then specifies consumer preference and product acceptability criteria. Operating in the realm of great uncertainty, marketing relays its requirements to a research organization, which further develops the initial concepts, still within the realm of uncertainty. Product development results are then conveyed to an engineering organization for clarification and development of product specifications. Through product, facilities, and process engineering disciplines, the product concepts are further quantified. Finally, detailed specifications within the limitations of actual resources are given to a production organization for fabrication. Throughout this process, a further clarification of concepts at each stage reduces uncertainty and the need for trade-offs.

Within this planning framework, planning can improve as information specifications get better. At the beginning of the process,

EXHIBIT 4.   PRODUCTION

ERA	PLANNING AND CONTROL NEEDS	DISTINGUISHING CHARACTERISTICS	CLASSICAL TECHNIQUES TO SATISFY			REASON FOR FAILURE	NEXT GENERATION TECHNIQUES	
			PLANNING	CONTROL			TECHNIQUES	PROPERTIES
				MONITOR	CORRECTIVE ACTION			
PERFORMANCE	COST	High-volume production Pricing structure used in standardized products	Budgets Manpower planning Estimating	Direct-labor standards Standard cost system	Breakeven analysis Reestimating	Lack of flexibility Costs by individual tasks needed Should be related to time Not predictive	Learning curve	Predictive Takes into account large variability in man-hours Projects cost in stable production situations
	SCHEDULE	Repetitive production Sales forecast Coordination Standard times required Machine loading	Gantt chart Production planning systems	Gantt chart Production control systems	Inventory control system	Lack of flexibility Constraints not indicated Uncertainty Should be related to cost Can be used only on production-oriented programs	Line of balance Milestone method Linear programming	Indicates events Constraints related to cost Based on standard times Schedules minimum inventory not ELS Milestones indicated on Gantt chart
	PERFORMANCE	High-volume production Coordination with engineering Quality control	Engineering specifications Blueprints Industry standards	Statistical quality control	Statistical quality control	Should be related to time and cost		
	INFORMATION	Manual development Need for operating information		Periodic reports Meetings	Periodic reports Meetings	Rapid information feedback required High cost	EAM systems	Processing of large amounts of data Rapid feedback

when information specifications are few, the demands of costs, schedule, and performance are most intensive. It is at this point that interfaces between organizations merge and the need for planning and control skills is the greatest. It is during this first stage in the process from consumer needs to final production that some measure of planning and program effectiveness is needed. Some of these measures are risk analysis, simulation of outcomes, and market research.

As they relate to planning, production programs are highly repetitive and therefore, as previously pointed out, have basically simple planning and control requirements. Engineering and marketing programs, however, are one-time-through programs, each one unique to its own technical and product development requirements. This difference stresses the need for general and adaptive planning models to be used as the basis of program development. In addition, this difference stresses the need for higher planning skills and a better understanding of the planning concept.

Throughout the evolution of planning and control techniques from production to engineering to marketing, four basic planning and control factors affect management decision making in each of these functional areas: time, cost, performance, and information. Each of these factors is related to one another and must be considered in the development of any planning and control system. The evolution of classical planning and control techniques will now be developed in terms of these four factors as they lead to the systems requirements of new product development programs.

PRODUCTION-ORIENTED CLASSICAL MANAGEMENT TECHNIQUES

Production-oriented organizations have a requirement for the planning and control of *cost*. (See Exhibit 4.) They are characterized by high-volume production of standardized products or at least products with an established bill of materials and associated standard costs. Frederick W. Taylor and his disciples, by observation and measurement, firmly established the concept of direct labor standards and control of direct labor costs. This basic approach evolved into such management system applications as measured piecework in repetitive factory operations.

It is important to emphasize that the concept of measuring direct labor costs in relation to volume of goods produced provided the central framework of cost control systems until the era of modern planning and control systems. The introduction of standard-cost and flexible-budget systems along with breakeven analysis during the 1920's depended upon this basic concept.

In these systems costs are segregated into the categories of "direct variable," "semivariable," and "fixed" with respect to volume of goods produced. In order for such cost control systems to be effective or valid, the variable cost must be based on data established by industrial engineering practices. The fixed or overhead elements in such cost control systems are generally handled on a budgeted basis; that is, annual levels of expenditure are determined, generally by functional or organizational units. With the introduction of work measurement techniques in the late 1940's, the practice of examining individual *overhead* tasks was established using, once again, industrial engineering techniques in determining direct cost measurement.

Given a pricing structure and a sales forecast of goods produced, these approaches to cost and profit control worked very well for the majority of American businesses through World War II and into the early 1950's.

However, as needs changed during the postwar period, these techniques were found lacking. The reasons for their failure to satisfy the needs of planning and control of cost were that

1. They lacked the flexibility required by modern programs.
2. Costs were needed by individual tasks.
3. Techniques did not have cost related to time.
4. None of the techniques was predictive.

Production-oriented organizations must control *schedules*. The distinguishing characteristic of scheduling in a production-oriented organization is that a schedule is based on

1. High-volume production of standardized products.
2. A sales forecast.
3. Standard times for the production of each unit.
4. Machine-loading constraints.
5. Coordination of various production departments.

A classical scheduling technique going back to the era of scientific management was the system introduced by Henry L. Gantt during

World War I. The distinguishing feature of this planning tool, the *Gantt chart*, is that work planned and work done are shown in their relation to each other and to time. Gantt charts (Exhibit 5) emphasize that time is the most important element in production. Gantt's approach also rests on the foundation of standard times—relatively certain estimated times for setup and processing. Gantt himself recognized the difficulty of obtaining realistic time estimates when standards are not available. His approach is not explicit on loading or other constraints upon starts and completions of individual tasks. This is understandable in terms of the well-structured production situation in which the Gantt chart is used. Finally, the Gantt chart is not generally used in any explicit manner for developing program costs by individual tasks.

It is important to emphasize, however, that the Gantt chart is widely used in many different versions. Until the advent of PERT, it represented the basic approach in planning not only production but all types of industrial effort. It continues to be used on development-oriented programs in two ways. First, it is used for overall *master planning* or schedule phasing, in which broad calendar-time goals for such a program are initially laid out. Second, it is used to provide summary information.

In addition to the previously listed limitations of the Gantt chart, production-based scheduling systems lacked flexibility, were not related to cost, did not reflect uncertainty, and were usable only on production-oriented programs.

Production-oriented organizations must also control *performance* —product performance in use, product reliability, and product maintainability. In a high-volume production organization, the distinguishing characteristic of performance is the necessity for coordination with engineering and quality control organizations.

Planning for performance in production-oriented organizations is generally accomplished through the preparation of design specifications, engineering specifications, and blueprints and sometimes through the use of industry standards. Control in performance is generally through inspection and statistical quality control.

The main reason for the failure of these techniques in modern programs is that performance factors are not related to time and cost of overall programs.

During World War II, improvements in the planning and control

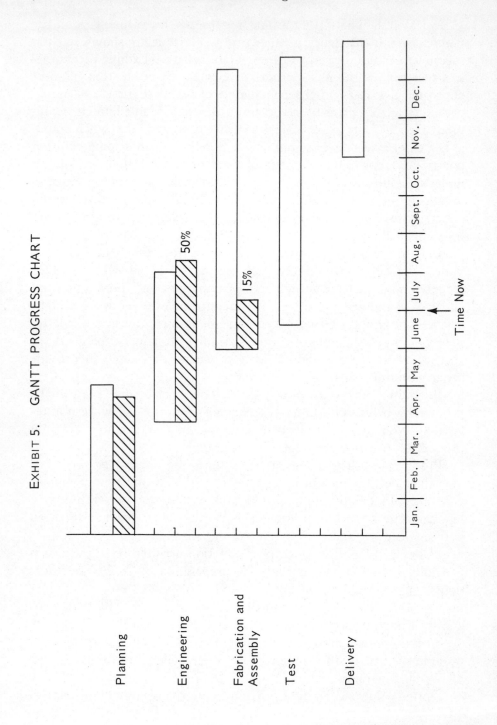

EXHIBIT 5. GANTT PROGRESS CHART

area were developed but were generally confined to production situations involving a medium range of volume. These developments involved the production of new materials (such as tanks, airplanes, radars, and electronic components) on a non-assembly-line basis.

These new developments included the line of balance technique, the learning curve technique, and the milestone method (which are discussed in the next section). Each made an important contribution, but other significant developments during the 1950's helped provide the foundation for new management planning and control systems. These included the development of *operations research* as a recognized management science. From operations research came approaches to developing models, both graphically and through the application of mathematical techniques. In industrial applications of operations research, the introduction of the flow model or *process diagram* became quite common. In addition, operations research or statistical approaches to the *probabilistic nature* of many industrial operations became an established concept, particularly in the areas of quality control and queuing theory. Last and by no means least was the development of an actual or *in-place business electronics data processing capability*.

ENGINEERING-ORIENTED CLASSICAL MANAGEMENT TECHNIQUES

Engineering-oriented development programs represent the next step in the evolution of planning and control techniques. (See Exhibit 6.) The requirements of World War II and the Cold War placed unique demands on business organizations and created one-time-through programs of a limited production nature, great complexity, and a high degree of technical and engineering content.

Engineering-oriented programs require the planning and control of *cost*. The distinguishing characteristics of planning and control of cost in an engineering program are the following:

1. Few units are produced.
2. Costs should decrease for each unit produced.
3. Preliminary cost estimating is required.
4. Cost should be coordinated with the schedule.

EXHIBIT 6.　ENGINEERING

ERA	PLANNING AND CONTROL NEEDS	DISTINGUISHING CHARACTERISTICS	CLASSICAL TECHNIQUES TO SATISFY			REASON FOR FAILURE	NEXT GENERATION TECHNIQUES	
			PLANNING	CONTROL			TECHNIQUES	PROPERTIES
				MONITOR	CORRECTIVE ACTION			
ENGINEERING	COST	Low volume Cost decrease per unit Preliminary estimating required Coordinate with scheduling	Budgets Line of balance Cost estimates	Estimates Line of balance	Variance analysis Re-estimating Line of balance	Difficulty of estimating cost with uncertainty in program Control techniques not available Not predictive Standard cost required Cost overruns	PERT/cost Value engineering Systems engineering	Predictive Controllable Clear definition Cost effectiveness
	SCHEDULE	Development-oriented One-time-through planning required Uncertainty Change Complexity Low volume Concurrency Optimize resources	Gantt chart Line of balance Milestone charts	Line of balance	Line of balance	Difficulty of estimating time with uncertainty in program High degree of program change Not predictive Standard times required Schedule slippages Multiple responsibilities Interdependency	PERT/time Configuration management; or systems engineering Program management Project definition	Predictive Integrative Interdependency Criticaliness Alternatives Objectives Optimize resources Flexible Corrective action
	PERFORMANCE	High engineering control High technical uncertainty Scarce resources Clear object Concurrency High production quality and acceptance test requirements	Design specifications Qualification specifications Acceptance specifications Reliability test specifications	Statistical quality control Configuration control	Statistical quality control	Lack of objectives High degree of program change Not predictive	Configuration management Work breakdown structure Systems engineering PERT/reliability	Change control Perform objectives Cost effectiveness Program definition
	INFORMATION	Time Cost Performance data needed Timeliness Diversity of activities Exception reporting	Line of balance	Line of balance Management information systems		Batch processing Slow response Limited capabilities	EDP system	Real time Rapid turnaround Exception reporting Can handle large number of transactions

Classical techniques to satisfy the cost needs for planning and control of engineering programs are budgets and cost estimates. A budget is a financial plan of action for a program covering a definite period of time. Cost estimates are based on judgment, known engineering data, and certain technical assumptions.

The reasons that these techniques have not been successful are these:

1. There is the great difficulty of estimating cost in programs with a high degree of technical uncertainty.
2. Cost planning and control techniques in engineering programs have not been available.
3. These classical techniques are not predictive.
4. Standard times are required for the classical techniques, yet engineering programs have great uncertainty.
5. These techniques cannot control cost overruns.

In the early 1950's, a new approach to the evaluation of costs was developed called value analysis or value engineering. It is an organized creative approach which efficiently identifies unnecessary costs.[8] In value engineering, unnecessary costs are defined as those costs which do not contribute to the function of the product or service. Value engineering approaches the problem from the basis of the cost of a product in dollars as related to the function secured from these dollars. It shows how to analyze accurately the functions of a product, identify what is desired, and place upon each function an appropriate cost. Because every dollar expense of every nature is intended by the purchaser to buy some type of function, this *function-based* system is applicable to all products and services.

Value analysis serves all branches of an enterprise: manufacturing, engineering, procurement, marketing, management. It results in the development of applicable specific information from the practically limitless stores of industrial technical information and skill for use in providing better value—that is, lower costs for appropriate products and services. It is a creative fact-finding process which is useful in minimizing costs at all stages of a product life cycle from before-the-fact cost avoidance work to after-the-fact cost reduction work.

[8] See Lawrence D. Miles, *Techniques of Value Analysis and Engineering* (New York: McGraw-Hill Book Company, 1961), p. 1.

Applying value engineering to new products is more difficult than is applying it to established products; different goals have to be set for the study, which has to be conducted in an organized and structured manner. In fact, to be really effective, value engineering has to be integrated into the process of developing a new product and must involve the major functions of the enterprise. The developmental process can be made much more efficient if good coordination can be obtained from the outset.

With a new product, the demand on value engineering can be great. In the first stage, the outline of the product may not be too accurate, particularly if no competitive product exists. The value-engineering work will have as its objective the development of a list of possible functions with an estimated cost. New ideas for functions must be developed and the effort for a new product requires real creative thinking. The final decision is generally a marketing responsibility, but the part played by value engineering is important.

Engineering-oriented programs have a requirement for the planning and control of *schedules*. The distinguishing characteristics of planning and control of schedules in an engineering program are that

1. They are development-oriented.
2. They are generally one-time-through programs.
3. Detailed planning is required.
4. There is a great deal of uncertainty.
5. There is a great deal of change.
6. They are highly complex programs.
7. Few units are produced.
8. There is a high degree of concurrency or overlap among the development, engineering, and production phases.
9. Resources must be optimized.

Classical techniques to satisfy the schedule planning and control needs of engineering programs are *Gantt charts* (see Exhibit 5), *milestone charts*, and the *line of balance* technique.

After World War II, the navy evolved the *milestone method* as another step toward a comprehensive program planning and control system. In essence, this approach represents a refinement of the Gantt chart method, as can be seen in Exhibit 7. In order to obtain a more detailed view of program status, individual "milestones" are called out within each horizontal bar on the Gantt chart. To be able to

EXHIBIT 7.   GANTT MILESTONE CHART

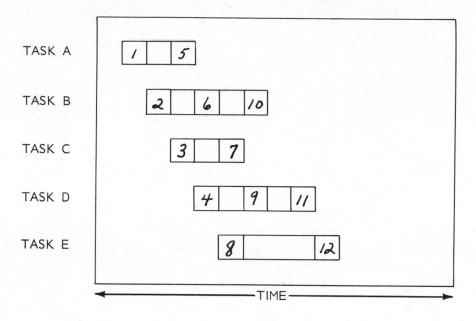

TIME

PERT NETWORK DERIVED

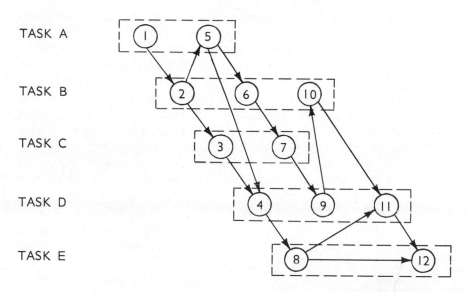

monitor program progress with any improved degree of success, these milestones must represent a carefully defined point in time; this is comparable to the PERT concept of an event.

The milestone method does not explicitly indicate the constraints that exist in the program. If these constraints were shown, as indicated in the bottom half of Exhibit 7, a milestone PERT network would be devised. Historically, there is no concept of resource allocation or costing directly related to the milestone method. By the mid-1950's it was realized that a better analytical approach would be required to give any validity or predictive quality to the milestone method. Like the Gantt chart, it has therefore tended to become a master scheduling or summary reporting technique.

Among scheduling techniques, *line of balance* is relatively old. It was developed around 1940 by the Goodyear Tire and Rubber Company for use as a scheduling and control technique. In the 1950's it was modified for use as a scheduling tool for development projects. There are four essential parts to a line of balance chart:

1. The *objective* is a curve which depicts planned cumulative expenditures. Another curve is related to it to depict actual expenditures. The curves may depict expenditures of man-hours, material, or money. Exhibit 8 (top left) is an example of an objective curve. The vertical axis represents cumulative expenditures and the horizontal axis represents time.

2. The *plan* is a time-phased chart depicting the occurrence of milestones and their interdependencies. (See Exhibit 8.)

3. *Progress* is usually indicated with a vertical bar graph. Exhibit 8 (top right) is an example of a line of balance progress chart. The height of the bar may indicate the relative progress of a phase of the project in terms of a percentage. For example, if, at a given point in time, a phase is 80 percent complete (rather than a planned 100 percent complete), the bar representing progress for this phase will be only four-fifths as high as it could be. The progress bar may also represent units, man-hours, or money.

4. The line of balance itself in Exhibit 8 represents expected progress for any given point in time. This is the horizontal line extending across the progress chart from the intersection of a vertical line with the objective curve. In this case, the line of balance represents the planned amount of money to be spent on each phase of each milestone by a given point in time.

EXHIBIT 8.   PROJECT LINE OF BALANCE DISPLAY

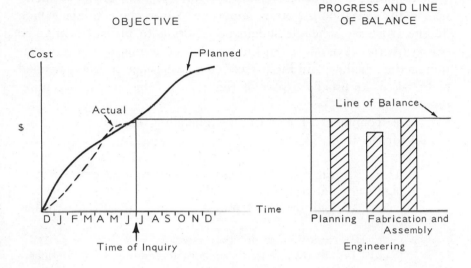

OBJECTIVE

PROGRESS AND LINE
OF BALANCE

PLAN

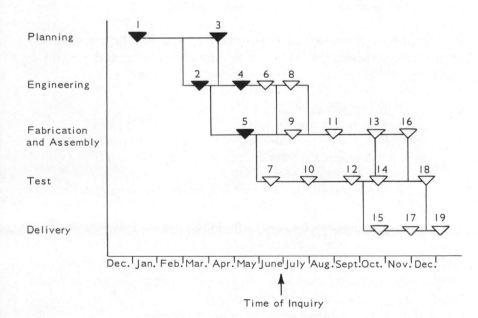

One additional significant part of the line of balance concept which should be mentioned is the *deviation report*. The philosophy behind the deviation report is important: Only those things which deviate from the schedule should be reported to management. The reason for the deviation from the schedule, the impact of the deviation on the schedule, and the corrective action taken or recommended to be taken are usually a part of this report. This is true exception reporting.

These techniques of engineering scheduling have not been successful for the following reasons:

1. There is great difficulty in estimating time in programs with a high degree of technical uncertainty.
2. There is a high degree of program change because of schedule slippage.
3. Classical techniques are not predictive.
4. Standard times are required for classical techniques, yet engineering programs have great uncertainty.
5. Engineering programs generally involve multiple responsibility for many activities.
6. There is a great deal of interdependency in engineering programs which classical techniques cannot handle.

Engineering-oriented programs have a need for the planning and control of performance. What distinguishes planning and control of performance in an engineering program is that they have

1. High engineering and technical content.
2. High technical uncertainty.
3. Scarce or limited resources; for example, manpower.
4. A requirement for clear objectives.
5. A high degree of concurrency.
6. High production quality and acceptance test requirements.

Classical techniques to satisfy the performance *planning* needs of engineering programs include design, qualification, acceptance, and reliability test specifications. Classical techniques which satisfy the performance control needs of engineering programs are statistical quality control and configuration control.

Configuration control is an established practice in industry under the name of engineering change control. Configuration in this context refers to identification of the product through formally prepared drawings. Configuration control refers to the specific procedures by which any changes in these drawings are proposed, approved, recorded, and distributed. Because configuration control, in a classical sense, begins at a point where drawings have been released to production, these procedures are usually highly formalized and comprehensive. The point at which approved drawings are available for release to production is the *base-line configuration point*. In an ideally executed program, the establishment of the base-line configuration occurs *after* prototypes of the product have been fabricated, assembled, and tested. In crash programs or in programs with a high degree of concurrency (where development and production are overlapped) the base-line configuration and the release of drawings to production may occur *prior to* prototype testing.

After the base-line design configuration point has been reached and drawings have been released to production, expenditures for procuring production materials, tooling, and establishing special production and testing facilities go up very rapidly. In addition, expenditures are also being incurred on the preparation of sales and advertising material, such as data sheets and product brochures. Hence the necessity for a highly structured approach in any established configuration or change control system, including a specialized drawing and change document numbering system and the review and approval of many individuals throughout the organization.

These techniques of performance planning and control in engineering-oriented programs have not been successful because

1. Performance requirements are generally not integrated into time and cost requirements in engineering programs.
2. There is a high degree of program change which classical techniques are not designed to handle.
3. The problems of concurrency cannot be integrated into classical techniques.
4. Classical techniques are not predictive.

Development-oriented programs have unique characteristics which have a very important bearing on effective performance planning and control; these include the special roles of systems engineering, reliability engineering (through PERT/reliability), and value engineering, as well as the fact that low unit volume generally is involved.

Information requirements of engineering-oriented programs are characterized by the urgent need for time, cost, and performance data. In addition, engineering programs have a great diversity of activities from which data are received; they require exception reporting; and they have problems of coordination and communication.

The line of balance technique satisfies some of these needs but not all of them. The capability of computers has only recently been explored to handle the specific planning and control problems of engineering programs. Up until now the batch processing requirements, slow response, and limited capabilities of electric accounting machines (EAM) have restricted the information needs of planning and control of engineering programs.

From operations research techniques developed in the 1950's and 1960's and through increased capabilities of computers came the next generation of planning and control techniques. These included PERT/time, PERT/cost, systems engineering, PERT/reliability, work breakdown structure concepts, project definition concepts, and program management, which are discussed in Chapter 3. Two additional techniques, value engineering and configuration management, have already been explored. Applied to one-time-through engineering-oriented programs, these techniques added another dimension to planning and control concepts and accomplished results that were undreamed of years before.

MARKETING-ORIENTED CLASSICAL MANAGEMENT TECHNIQUES

Marketing programs, specifically in new product development, are much broader in their scope than production- and engineering-based programs. (See Exhibit 9.) This is because a new product development program must include not only the specific requirements of production and engineering, but also those of research and development, purchasing, vendors, all the various marketing organizations, and many others. Marketing is basically an intellectual and creative process and is relatively difficult to plan because of uncertainty. The diverse organizational needs of new product development programs—from the quantified variables of production to the

EXHIBIT 9. MARKETING, RESEARCH, AND DEVELOPMENT

ERA	PLANNING AND CONTROL NEEDS	DISTINGUISHING CHARACTERISTICS	CLASSICAL TECHNIQUES TO SATISFY			REASON FOR FAILURE	NEXT GENERATION TECHNIQUES	
			PLANNING	CONTROL			TECHNIQUES	PROPERTIES
				MONITOR	CORRECTIVE ACTION			
MARKETING, RESEARCH, AND DEVELOPMENT	COST	Program definition required; High risk; High degree of change; Much interface; Should be integrated with schedule and performance; Flexibility	Cost estimates; Budgets; Long-range plan	Budget; Status reporting; Updating; Meetings	Re-estimating	Programs complex; High degree of change; High risk; Not responsive; Not flexible; Criticalness not indicated; Not predictive; Interdependent	Product development planning and control system (PDPCS)	Predictive; Integrative; Interdependence; All activities shown; Criticalness; Alternatives indicated; Risk analysis; Simulation; Program definition; Resource allocation; Responsive; Automatic updating; Automatic replanning; Controllable; Hierarchy of detail; Immediate status information; Rapid turnaround time; Program management organization; Uncertainty understandable
	SCHEDULE	Program definition required; Planning required; Complexity; Uncertainty; High risk; Concurrency change; Much interface; One-time-through; Integrated with cost; Performance; Change	PERT/time; Gantt charts; Long-range plan	Schedule status; Reporting; Updating; Meetings	Replanning	Not responsive; Coordination not efficient; Complex concurrency; Not flexible; Sophisticated system not understood; Limited resources; Criticalness not indicated; Change not predictive; Interdependent risk	Product development planning and control system (PDPCS)	
	PERFORMANCE	Extensive R & D required; Clear goals required; Concurrency; Extensive product testing; Should be integrated with time/cost change; Complexity	Concept testing; Market research; Concept definition; Engineering specifications	Product testing	Statistical quality control	Not easily or clearly defined; High risk; Concurrency; Not predictive; High degree of program change; Interdependent; Criticalness; Complexity	Product development planning and control system (PDPCS)	
	INFORMATION	Required by diverse organizations; Timeliness; Coordination required; Exception reporting	Committees; Reports; Meetings	Committees; Reports; Meetings		EDP system not used extensively in marketing; Too sophisticated; Criticalness	Product development planning and control system (PDPCS)	

difficulties of creative planning of marketing—indicate that an integrated planning and control system specifically designed for new product development programs is urgently needed. For the purposes of this discussion, a new product development program is the activities which occur after actual go-ahead for development. We are *not* concerned with the development of a marketing plan, from idea search, concept development, or preliminary economic analysis to development go-ahead. What does concern us are the characteristics of marketing-oriented new product development programs and the classical management techniques used to plan and control them.

Marketing programs have some distinguishing characteristics that are common to the planning and control needs of time, cost, and performance. These include

1. The need to define objectives.
2. Great uncertainty in marketing programs.
3. High risk in marketing programs.
4. High degree of program change.
5. Interface and interdependency between organizations.
6. The need for flexibility.
7. One-time-through programs.

In marketing programs, *cost* should always be integrated with time and performance. Additional *schedule* characteristics include the need for a fully detailed marketing program and great program complexity. *Performance* characteristics to be added are extensive research and development and product testing requirements.

The distinguishing characteristics of information needs include the following:

1. Adequate information regarding program status is required by all organizations involved.
2. Information must be timely, almost real time.
3. Coordination and communication are required.
4. Exception reporting is necessary.

Planning and control of *cost* in marketing programs are generally accomplished through a sequence of three approaches. Early in the planning of new products, long-range plans are prepared which, among other things, project new product costs one, five, or as much as ten years into the future. These costs obviously are rough "guessti-mates" and establish an order of magnitude for management con-sideration. As new product projects are established, preliminary cost estimates are generally prepared by research, engineering, purchasing, manufacturing, and marketing groups. These estimates tend to be "quick and dirty" because at this stage in a new product project greater accuracy may not be warranted. As a project progresses, cost estimates are refined and eventually used as one basis for a "go" de-cision by management. From this point in a program, departmental or cost center budgets are prepared in order to control costs.

Most marketing plans include budgets of marketing costs by various classifications. The objective of these budgets is to indicate the plan of expenditures of marketing funds over time and to control the expenditures through periodic analysis of discrepancies for reme-dial action. A basic assumption to this approach is that expenditures either under or over the budgeted figures are significant to manage-ment.

These techniques are obviously unable to satisfy the cost charac-teristics of marketing and development programs. They do not ade-quately cope with marketing program complexity, risk, and uncer-tainty; they are not responsive to marketing needs and the high degree of program change. They also are not flexible, do not indi-cate critical aspects of a program, and are not predictive. Nor do they indicate the organizational interdependencies that exist in a marketing program. Obviously, new approaches are needed.

Schedule planning and control in marketing programs are two of the major problems in marketing management. Programs involving products which have been on the market for some time are easier to schedule because of accumulated experience by marketing managers. However, with really new products that involve new technology or new markets, the tendency of marketing executives has been to go slowly and accumulate experience as they move along. It is this tend-ency that accounts for the excessively long lead times and high failure rate of new products. It is because marketing managers prefer to "feel their way" in market development that plans and schedules are inadequate or nonexistent. In those cases where commitments can be obtained, the only schedule is a master schedule that indicates major milestone events. These schedules are prepared in Gantt chart form from which graphic displays can be presented for top management review.

Only recently have network analysis techniques been utilized to schedule marketing programs. There is evidence that, where network analysis is used, the only aspect of the technique that is utilized is the network itself and not its other capabilities.

Coordination and control of marketing programs are most often obtained through various devices. The master schedule focuses attention on the time element. Clearances by higher executives for the initiation of certain activities and for expenditures are informative. Initialing of memoranda indicating agreement with ideas or procedures is a device often used, but it can tend to slow down operations. Staff meetings are held by most concerns for threshing out important matters, for expediting them, and for exchanging information. Progress and status reports are often required so that periodic analyses of program status can be made for those involved. Once again, for the same reasons that they cannot cope with the cost problems involved, these approaches inadequately satisfy the needs of new product program schedules.

The planning of performance criteria in marketing-based development programs is through such classical techniques as concept definition and concept testing through market research and through engineering specifications. Control of marketing program performance is obtained through product testing and statistical quality control. These techniques are inadequate in satisfying the needs of dynamic marketing-based product development programs for much the same reasons that they do not satisfy scheduling or cost needs.

In product development programs, the needed information is generally obtained through committee meetings and status reports, neither of which satisfies the planning and control requirements. Only recently have there been indications that marketing executives in major firms are interested in utilizing electronic data processing systems to provide information on marketing programs. The gains to be achieved are phenomenal.

Classical techniques for planning and control of schedules and performance have failed to satisfy the needs of marketing programs because they cannot efficiently coordinate such programs. These programs have concurrency and limited resources available, and where network analysis has been used, either it was too sophisticated a tool or it was not understood.

Out of the unique requirements of new product development programs for a planning and control system, an integrated approach has evolved which is discussed in Chapter 4. However, before such a system can be described, we must first indicate some organizational approaches to product development and then review the system requirements necessary for product development programs.

ORGANIZATIONAL APPROACHES TO PRODUCT DEVELOPMENT PROGRAMS

One of the most common organizational approaches to product development is the new product committee—a means of administering and controlling a new product development project. The major benefit of a new product committee is its usefulness as a communication device, an advisory device, a means of screening ideas, and a means of planning. On the other hand, new product committees have certain limitations. Experience indicates that if a committee is established or, in fact, seeks to act as a substitute for individual responsibility and initiative in regard to new product problems, it will be ineffective. A committee cannot evaluate new product decisions without adequate preliminary staff work. Another danger is the pressure toward conformity created by the presence of strong personalities or an opinionated chairman. Other limitations include problems of absenteeism, changing membership, and lack of adequate understanding by all participants.

One approach toward coordinating new product development programs by a product planning committee is the product development progress chart (see Exhibit 10). This chart indicates pertinent information about each new product program reviewed by a product planning committee including project number, priority, project description, project team members, latest meeting dates, and dates of key events in each program. Used by the product planning committee at American Standard Inc. in New York, the product development progress chart enables management to monitor its new product development programs.[9]

Another popular approach to coordinating and controlling prod-

[9] Robert W. Lear, "The Product Planning Committee: Its Opportunities and Responsibilities," *Establishing a New Product Program*, AMA Management Report No. 8, p. 57.

EXHIBIT 10.   PRODUCT DEVELOPMENT PROGRESS CHART

Group: *Gas Heating Agenda*   Date: *Dec. 15, 1957*

Agenda Placement		Project No.	Announcement Goal Date	Project Description	Project Team	Date Appointed	Latest Meeting	Preliminary Design Specs. Submit	Final Design Specs. Submit Date	Estimated Release Date to Mfg.	Product Avail.
Date	Priority										
1/1/57	1	RH-43	3/1/58	Redesign Residential Boiler	S. Smith M. Brown R. Jones	1/11/57	9/30/57	4/16/57	9/22/57	11/1/57	4/1/58
								Actual	Actual		

uct development programs is the use of a new products department or product planning department. This approach has grown rapidly during the past decade. According to a research study of more than 200 companies, 86 percent had formal new product departments. This shows a significant increase from 56 percent of companies surveyed in 1960 and 22 percent of those surveyed in 1956.

This survey disclosed that the formalization of new product departments came about as a result of an evolutionary process. Initially, the chief executive, strongly led by R&D, made practically all the decisions from start to finish. In time, the executive committee became active. As the workload increased, a subcommittee was established to deal with the evaluation and coordination of new products. As the coordination problem became more complex and unwieldy, the next logical step was to form a new products department with one man in charge of directing and coordinating the job for top management.[10]

The duties of a new product department divide into two possible kinds of work—deciding what to do and deciding how to do it. Typically these responsibilities include

1. Recommending new product objectives and program.
2. Planning exploratory activities.
3. Making screening decisions.
4. Developing specifications.
5. Recommending development of new products.
6. Coordinating testing and precommercialization.
7. Directing interdepartmental teams at all levels.

The new products department is generally considered to be an organizing force in a company. Its basic job is to get the resources of the company coordinated against the development of the new product. Since a new product program must not only reflect corporate objectives, but integrate its output into corporate activities, new products departments generally report to a top executive. Positioning a new product department directly under the president insures total corporate coordination.

In those companies where executives feel that the authority and responsibility for new product coordination should be vested in a

[10] *Management of New Products* (New York: Booz, Allen & Hamilton Inc., 1964), 4th edition, p. 20.

single individual, the product-manager system is a feasible alternative. This system of coordination involves spreading out product assignments in a company among several product managers.[11] In what might be called the conventional use of a product manager, one man may be placed in charge of a new item soon after the product idea is approved. He serves as this product's "guardian angel" throughout all phases of its life cycle. Under this arrangement, a product manager may be appointed for each new product, or else a new product is simply assigned to a regular product manager whose existing line is most closely related to it.

Another arrangement is to put one of the company's product managers in sole charge of coordinating the early development stages of every new product. When a product is established in the market, responsibility for its management can then be transferred to a regular manager.

The assignment of responsibility for a product to a product manager carries with it the necessity for providing authority as well as the equipment, the personnel, and the money to go with it. The product-manager concept works best when top management support and the necessary tools are provided.

[11] For a discussion of the product-manager concept and its use, see the Conference Board Report, *The Product-Manager System*, Experiences in Marketing Management No. 8 (New York: National Industrial Conference Board, 1965).

2

Systems Requirements for
Planning and Control of
Product Development Programs

TWO MAJOR DIMENSIONS of new products have been identified—technology and markets. Now a third is added—product evolution, or the time it takes to bring a product into existence. Exhibit 11 illustrates this dimension. As indicated by the arrow, a new products program begins with company objectives, which include product fields of interest, profit aims, and growth plans. The more specifically these objectives can be drawn, the greater the guidance that will be provided to the programs. The concept of objectives is to be covered in more detail later in this chapter when planning requirements of new product programs are explored. In Chapter 4, formal recognition of the objectives concept will be explored in the project definition phase of the planning and control system to be developed.

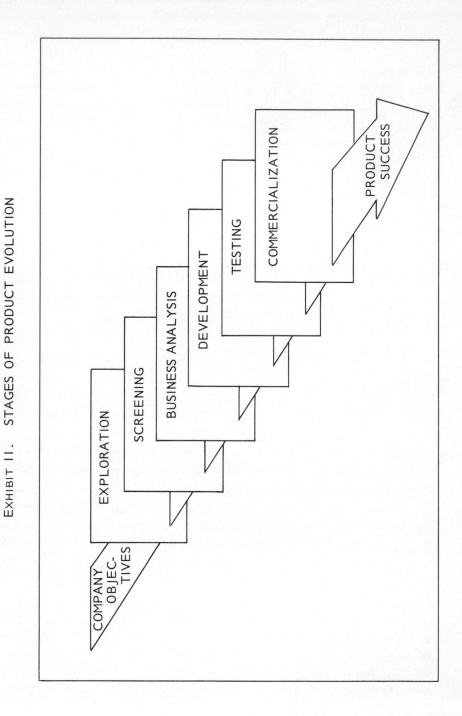

EXHIBIT II. STAGES OF PRODUCT EVOLUTION

COMPANY OBJEC-TIVES

EXPLORATION

SCREENING

BUSINESS ANALYSIS

DEVELOPMENT

TESTING

COMMERCIALIZATION

PRODUCT SUCCESS

The Nature of Modern Product Development Programs

It should be clear by now that a new products program is a complex and often sizable activity which embraces the whole company. Such a complex activity must be broken down into functions and stages that can be managed, planned, and controlled. A six-stage pattern is most common and represents the basic management process before company, industry, organization, or product variations are considered. These six stages as shown in Exhibit 11 are

- *Exploration*—The search for product ideas to meet company objectives.
- *Screening*—A quick analysis to determine which ideas are pertinent and merit more detailed study.
- *Business analysis*—The expansion of the idea, through creative analysis, into a concrete business recommendation including product features and a program for the product.
- *Development*—The turning of the idea-on-paper into a product-in-hand, demonstrable and producible.
- *Testing*—The commercial experiments necessary to verify earlier business judgments.
- *Commercialization*—Launching the product in full-scale production and sale, committing the company's reputation and resources.

Exhibit 12 shows a more detailed approach to stages of product evolution in 33 steps of idea development along with pertinent comments about hardware-oriented product development.

The time span for product development varies very significantly among products and industries. Exhibit 13 shows the average of the fastest to slowest times, in months, of development activities from initial product conception to completion of market testing in the grocery products field. As can be seen, this time varies from a minimum of 14 months to a maximum of 87 months.

The decay curve for ideas is characteristic of the new product development process. As shown in Exhibit 14, this is represented by the progress of rejection of ideas or projects by stage in the new product process. Although the rate of rejection varies somewhat among industries and more markedly among companies, the general shape of

Exhibit 12. STEPS FROM IDEA TO PRODUCTION

1. <u>Product concept.</u> Basic product ideas are established and defined.

2. <u>Preliminary screening.</u> This initial appraisal eliminates product ideas which are obviously impractical or otherwise unacceptable.

3. <u>Patent search.</u> This search identifies controlling patents, licenses, and unprotected areas.

4. <u>Preliminary technical-economic survey.</u> General investigation assesses: practicability of the product, nature and size of market, sales methods, manufacturing requirements, management, personnel and organization requirements, profit potential (effect of taxes), and breadth of corporate charter.

5. <u>Literature search.</u> Available literature relating to the product concept and the market should be reviewed and pertinent data accumulated.

6. <u>Final screening.</u> Acceptance or rejection of ideas at this point is based upon findings of the literature search, preliminary technical-economic survey, and the patent search.

7. <u>Project scheduling.</u> The following must be assigned:

    Funds • Establish a budget adequate for development and preliminary market testing.

    Priority • Establish a timetable.

    Manpower • Establish an organization.

8. <u>Development of preliminary technical-economic survey.</u> This process should amplify investigation of subjects covered in the preliminary technical-economic survey and establish basic acceptability of product for commercial exploitation.

9. <u>Research.</u> Research must establish basic new principles and data related to the project.

10. <u>Development.</u> A preliminary model should be constructed.

11. <u>Engineering.</u> Sound principles of construction should be incorporated in the model.

12. <u>Management review and approval of pilot run.</u> Based upon available data, management should determine the advisability of a pilot run for the purpose of gathering additional manufacturing and marketing data.

13. <u>Design review.</u> Prior to a pilot run, the design should be reviewed to make certain that it incorporates the best features for performance, production, serviceability cost, and sales appeal.

14. Prototype model. A model is constructed which represents the product to be offered for sale.

15. Engineering tests. The prototype model is given a performance test in the engineering department.

16. Field tests. The prototype model is given a test under actual working conditions.

17. Review of test data. Test data are analyzed and designs are revised to improve performance, ease of manufacturing, serviceability, cost savings, and sales appeal.

18. Redesign. The prototype model is redesigned to incorporate new design features. Final product styling is also incorporated in the model at this point.

19. Production review and redesign. The design is reviewed and design modifications made to improve ease of production and to lower cost.

20. Final model. All final design modifications are incorporated in this model.

21. Preliminary production analysis. The design is processed for manufacturing.

22. Elements to be manufactured. Parts of the product to be manufactured by the corporation are selected.

23. Elements to be purchased. Parts and subassemblies of the product to be purchased are selected.

24. Realistic cost analysis. Manufacturing and purchased parts cost are estimated.

25. Pilot run. A small quantity of the product is produced to test manufacturing cost estimates and the marketing program.

26. Initial market test. The pilot run is marketed in a selected area for experimental and analytical purposes.

27. Management review and approval of production release. Results of the market test are examined by management. If the profit outlook appears favorable, production is released.

28. Service organization. Service facilities are organized.

29. Distribution organization. Distribution channels are organized.

30. Installation of general sales organization. The selling organization is installed along with service facilities.

31. Production tooling. Equipment, tools, gauges, and fixtures are made ready for production.

32. Production. Manufacture commences.

33. "Bread and butter" production and distribution. The product is manufactured and sold.

EXHIBIT 13. HOW LONG DOES IT TAKE TO INTRODUCE NEW PRODUCTS?

(Figures indicate time in average months)

	Initial Product Conception	Development of Satisfactory Product	Final Packaging Approval	Completion of Test Marketing	Full Production Readiness	Months of Trial Before Product Is Judged Failure or Success
Average of Fastest Times	3	2	2	1	3	3
Average Times	13	4	7	2	4	10
Average of Slowest Times	31	6	8	12	6	24

NOTE: July 1964 mail survey of 23 grocery product companies with total sales exceeding $10 billion.

Source: D. W. Twedt, "How Long Does It Take to Introduce New Products?" *Journal of Marketing* (January 1965), Vol. 29, pp. 71-72.

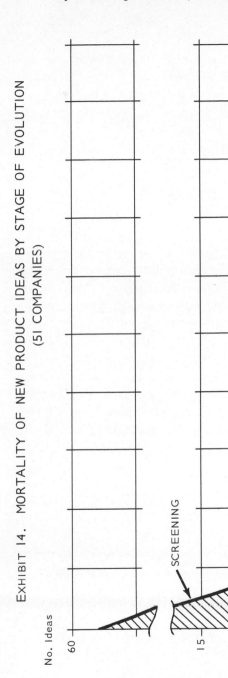

EXHIBIT 14. MORTALITY OF NEW PRODUCT IDEAS BY STAGE OF EVOLUTION (51 COMPANIES)

Source: *Management of New Products*, 4th edition, Management Research Department, Booz, Allen & Hamilton Inc., 1964.

the decay curve is typical. As will be noted, it takes some 58 ideas to yield one successful product.

Each stage of product evolution is progressively more expensive as measured in both time and money. Exhibit 15 shows the rate at which dollars are spent during the average project. This exhibit is illustrative of an industry average; the dotted line shows an all-industry average of capital expenditures concentrated in the last three stages of evolution.

PLANNING REQUIREMENTS OF NEW PRODUCT DEVELOPMENT PROGRAMS

The purpose of planning is to enable management to apply its resources most effectively toward the accomplishment of objectives. Planning is the process of making tentative decisions for future product-planning actions within the overall performance objectives of the organization. In addition, planning can be considered the clarification of objectives and the determination of what action must be taken, when, by whom, and at what cost in order to achieve specified goals.[1]

Despite the impossibility of accurately forecasting the future, the business planner *identifies* a range of possibilities and *prepares* for them. Once this is understood, the difference between planning and forecasting becomes clearer. "Forecasting" is attempting to find the most probable course of events or a range of probabilities. "Planning" is deciding what one will do about them.

PREREQUISITES OF GOOD PLANNING

As part of a discussion of planning requirements, seven prerequisites of good product development planning should be indicated.

1. Recognition of the need for planning.
2. Top management support.
3. Intelligent and enthusiastic participation of key personnel.
4. The establishment of some basic policies.

---

[1] Stewart Thompson, *How Companies Plan*, AMA Research Study No. 54 (New York: American Management Association, 1964), p. 13.

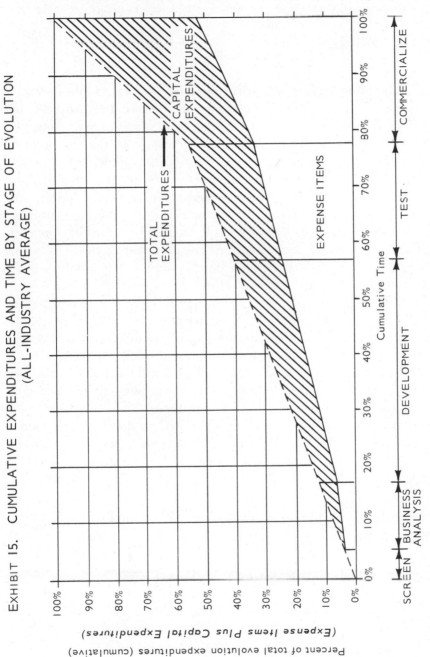

EXHIBIT 15. CUMULATIVE EXPENDITURES AND TIME BY STAGE OF EVOLUTION (ALL-INDUSTRY AVERAGE)

Percent of total evolution expenditures (cumulative)
(Expense Items Plus Capital Expenditures)

TOTAL EXPENDITURES

CAPITAL EXPENDITURES

EXPENSE ITEMS

Cumulative Time

SCREEN BUSINESS ANALYSIS DEVELOPMENT TEST COMMERCIALIZE

Source: Management Research Department, Booz, Allen & Hamilton Inc., 1964.

    5. The establishment of tentative assumptions and objectives.
    6. A systematic training program for managers in the planning procedures of the company.
    7. Planning procedures so simple that the average man can follow them without extensive training.

Recognition of the need is the first requirement. Unless there is an absolute, thorough understanding of the essential necessity for product development planning—not just as something it would be nice to do, but as something that absolutely *must* be done in order to solve major development problems—it will be difficult to engender enough support throughout an organization to get the job done.

The second requirement is top management support. Support must be available from the top of whatever echelon inaugurates product development planning. This does not necessarily mean that the support of the chairman of the board or the president of the company is necessary; good product development planning can be put into practice at an intermediate echelon.

The third prerequisite is that product development planning must have the intelligent and enthusiastic participation of key personnel. When responsibility is delegated to a product development manager or team member, it involves delegating the responsibility and authority to plan, to budget, to evaluate, and to execute. Therefore, down through an organization, from top to bottom, planning is an integral and essential part of managerial performance.

The fourth requirement is that basic product development policies be established. These policies should include such items as limitations on types of products to be marketed, procedural stages in development, specific responsibilities in product development, product line extension policy, acceptance and screening criteria for new products, acceptable sources of new product ideas, and acceptable search strategies. Financial considerations can also be included which may indicate investment limitations, return on investment and payoff procedures and criteria, and research and development expenditure policies. These policies should guide company product development activities and individual projects as soon as planning begins.

The fifth requirement is the establishment of tentative assumptions and objectives. Assumptions indicate the ground rules on which planning is based. They are necessary because all planning is subject to strategic uncertainties in the future. Objectives should be clearly defined, with specific goals indicated. A statement of objectives should include a description of scope in terms of activity and range of operation, restrictions, conditions, and decision points at which selections will be made from alternatives.

The sixth prerequisite is a training program. This program will first explain the plan for product development planning and then motivate individuals to do the job.

The seventh factor is a *simple* planning process. The plan for product development planning must be so simple that the average man can follow it without extensive training and in a limited time. Unless the average executive can do the planning required, it will be difficult to get him to carry it out.

TIME/COST/PERFORMANCE FACTORS OF PLANNING

Complex product development projects can be managed effectively when project managers have the means to plan and control the schedules and costs of the work required to achieve their objectives. The serious schedule slippages and cost overruns that have been experienced on many new product development programs indicate that managers at all levels need improved techniques at all stages in a project to

1. Define the work to be performed.
2. Develop more realistic schedule and cost estimates based on the resources planned to perform the work.
3. Determine where resources should be applied to best achieve the time, cost, technical performance, and other objectives.
4. Consider the risk and uncertainty in new product programs.
5. Indicate the interdependencies, interrelationships, and interfaces between tasks and organizations.
6. Integrate the requirements of diverse organizational units.
7. Consider the constraints existing in a program.

SETTING OBJECTIVES

There is a clear objective in selecting products for development: to pick the best ideas for investing available new product time and money. There are more high-risk than low-risk products; and there are more low-payout than high-payout ones. This fact sometimes leads to the belief that for an idea to have a high payout it must, *ipso facto*, have high risk. However, management's purpose is to find those rare ideas that have both low risk and high payout. This is the key to maximum yield on available manpower and resources.

The very existence of the company implies it has certain goals; this orientation is necessary for the formation of an integrated product planning system. The answers to questions regarding projected business activity, rate of growth, corporate direction, method of growth, image, and other objectives may provide an insight into a company's changing needs for the future. Planning is a means of anticipating and coping with such needs. Coping with a change suggests the existence of a preprogrammed package or of structural decisions relative to a set of actions or reactions available for immediate application.

Another more fundamental determinant of the success of new products is the extent to which they move the company in the desired direction. All the work of planning the introduction may have been misdirected if management has not first assured itself that each product on the launching ramp fits into an overall plan covering such factors as investment, profits, markets, product line goals, and the use of available strengths in the organization. One major function of a chief executive is to define the direction and limits of company growth. These definitions become major objectives of the firm. In this way, objectives serve to answer questions that arise from daily operations: What is to be achieved? At what rate? Which project has priority?

Before setting objectives for new product development there must be a thorough understanding of a firm's capabilities. These include the major resources available to management: money, machinery and equipment, space, materials, location, procedures, and methods. Most important of all, the capability of the firm is found in the knowledge of the technical specialists and managers and in their ability to turn this knowledge into commercially feasible projects.

The manager who is searching for new opportunities for growth should seek to define his business in terms of its specific capacities to perform—its own hard core of competence—as well as in terms of the industry in which the firm's capacity seems currently to fit.

The matters on which explicit assumptions regarding new product planning will be made are determined in part by the span of time involved. If a manager is concerned only with the immediate year or two ahead, then his assumptions may not be what they would be if he were trying to assess the impact of his decisions over a decade or a generation. One question that may bring to light a few assumptions on which a product plan may rest is this: What are the conditions that must exist if the plan is to be workable?

Objectives for specific product development activities should be the outgrowth of a firm's overall business plan. Objectives enable a manager to do at least three things: (1) to evaluate the merits of unforeseen opportunities when they occur, (2) to weigh alternative courses of action, and (3) to study his past and current practices so as to improve his performance. For each product development project, objectives should be clearly defined with specific goals indicated. (An objective is what should be accomplished at the end; a goal is what should be possible when the end is achieved.)

Existing conditions which restrict feasible action, the sequence points at which decisions will be made, and the alternatives available should be considered in establishing product development objectives. In addition, there should be a statement indicating the exceptions from company policy that apply to a particular program and an indication of the risks involved in attempting the development and marketing of the product. A further development of these objectives in terms of modern planning and control systems is described in Chapter 4.

SCHEDULING

A schedule is a plan or proposal for future procedure indicating the objective proposed and the time and sequence of each operation. Project scheduling, then, is arranging the distinguishable parts of an undertaking into a time sequence. For our purposes, a project is an organized undertaking with a defined end—perhaps the launching of a product into test market or the production of a product for national expansion.

To be effective, scheduling techniques must aid both management and those directly responsible for the work of a project, whether an engineer or an assembler on the production line. Managers need techniques which will provide schedules in which they can have confidence. These techniques should allow those working on a new product project to schedule their segment of the work and thus lead these people to think out and plan their work more thoroughly than they might otherwise do.

Scheduling techniques must focus attention on the work of any group which affects the work of other groups. These techniques should also show the timetable for the work and should enable management to monitor progress on it. Techniques should be relatively easy to use and should provide easily interpreted information. If they do not meet these requirements, they cannot be considered useful tools, regardless of their *potential* effectiveness. They are of additional value if they enable management to pre-evaluate alternative courses of action.

The sheer number of activities and people involved in a new product program, the variations in activity time, and the need for adherence to a predetermined time target make desirable the preparation and use of a schedule. Making one up is something like working a jigsaw puzzle, in that all the pieces become meaningful only when they are properly placed. Then the program can be seen as a whole by executives, and each participant can see how his specialized activity fits into the whole effort. The schedule should indicate not only *what* things are to be done and *when*, but also when activities must *start* if deadlines and milestones are to be met and *who* is responsible for each major activity. Without a schedule, group effort is likely to be haphazard, to say the least.

RESOURCE ALLOCATION

Resource allocation is the scheduled utilization of resources during a project. The resources to be scheduled include, in particular, men, machines, facilities, and materials. Money is initially involved in any consideration of resources, of course, since the desire to use resources efficiently grows from the need to keep costs as low as practical. Techniques for managing the allocation of resources are based on the premise that, within limits, trade-offs of time, men, facilities, and materials are possible in the scheduling and performance of a project.

Resource scheduling techniques can be used for individual product development projects as well as the overall resource scheduling for all product development projects within a division or company. Management would like, within reasonable bounds, to keep its total resource requirements from fluctuating too much. Resource scheduling helps them do this while considering such things as the schedules and priorities of all projects. One approach to this is to combine the schedules and resource requirements of all projects and to process these against the total resources available while considering the relative weights management has applied to such things as cost, stable personnel levels, and project priorities.

Resource allocation is an analytical tool designed to assist product development managers and others in the systematic development of the most efficient project plan—that is, a plan in which resources (men, equipment, and so on) are assigned to a project in such a way that the marketing and technical objectives are achieved at either the lowest cost for a specified time duration or in the shortest time within a specified cost limit. Whereas specialized techniques such as PERT are specifically intended for application in planning and controlling entire projects, resource allocation may be used effectively in planning a small group of associated activities that represent only a minor portion of the overall project.

Resource allocation techniques are based on the premise that tasks to be performed in a program, like total programs themselves, are subject to time-cost trade-offs. The techniques assume, in other words, that tasks or activities can be carried out in more than one way and that these alternative methods will produce different cost estimates and time durations.

Resource allocation techniques can be described briefly as follows:

1. Management first defines the project in terms of a detailed plan of activities (a network, for example) with complete specifications for the work to be performed. Alternative times and costs are then estimated for each of the activities. (Any number of meaningful time-cost combinations may be estimated.)
2. The duration of a task is initially set at the time associated with its lowest cost alternative. Then, by selecting shorter time/higher cost points on certain critical activities, time is "bought" until the project duration is equal to or slightly less than the target duration.

PROGRAM CONSTRAINTS

Plans are constrained by operational objectives. This means that the plans must be within the scope of the organization's resources and directed toward the stated objectives. Plans should be realistic: They should take into account the natural state of the environment and the conditions which are achievable within the range of available resources. "Available" is a key word here, as the resources not available to the product development program or under its jurisdiction are of no value.

Typical constraints to planning a product development project include company policy, the program budget, marketing strategy, company circumstances and long-range plans, and economic forecasts.

Company policies may act as a constraint to product development programs because they may establish the scope and range of development activity. Product development policies are a general guide to action and may indicate selection procedures; return on investment, volume, profit, and payout criteria; patent, copyright, and business protection requirements; quality, producibility, maintainability, reliability and safety guides; design, packaging, and pricing policy; and product line compatibility requirements.

The program budget restrains product development activity because it establishes economic limits. Companies tend to balance their research budgets against present sales or operating investments rather than anticipate opportunities or potential threats. In relating the budget to product development activity, two points should be remembered: (1) Product planning and research require greater investment risk than do the more certain projects of other organizational functions; and (2) the importance of a flexible budget lies in its ability to fund the unpredictable investment activities that are characteristic of research.

Marketing strategy restricts product development activity because it establishes the limits of marketing considerations. These limits, characterized by marketing analysis, insure that acceptable products are marketed to consumers. There are eight specific objectives of quantitative marketing analysis:

1. To determine whether to produce a product.
2. To determine the order of market development.

3. To determine how much to produce.
4. To determine where to place merchandise in the market.
5. To determine whether to expand production capacity.
6. To determine the location of new production capacity.
7. To determine the allocation of advertising and other promotional effort.
8. To determine the proper channels of distribution.

Each of these objectives can limit product development activity.

Company circumstances can also limit a new product project. Merger and acquisition activity, executive turnover, corporate expansion, limited production facilities, shortage of research personnel, and organizational changes occurring within a firm may be reasons for restricting development work.

Company long-range plans may also restrain product development work. These restraints are imposed by company requirements for stability, flexibility, growth capacity, and organizational balance. A long-range plan for new product development may include the time of formulation, expected time of completion of each project, the reason for the plan, and the organizational impact of its completion. The long-range plan insures that specifications from product planning, product development, and market-sector penetration and exploitation are realized to anticipate the company's present and future competitive obligations. More specifically, the long-range plan insures the effective transfer of technology from product planning to operations.

An economic forecast may limit development activity because it establishes the economic level at which the company can support product planning and the future economic climate which will be acceptable for the introduction of new products. An evaluation of the economic forecast enables an orientation of planning effort toward the long-range future while maintaining the proper perspective toward the immediate environment.

CONTROL REQUIREMENTS OF NEW PRODUCT DEVELOPMENT PROGRAMS

The central problem in organizing the activities of new product development programs is the establishment of criteria by which to guide the work and determine progress. The activity of new product development generally involves a large number of participants working on different parts of the same project. This multiplicity of effort suggests that new product development must be coordinated, with each member responsible and, at the same time, creative. The complexity and cost of most product development projects, coupled with the requirements of evaluation, demand that the project be laid out in advance. Pre-established time schedules and budgets for the project must be adhered to. Additional requirements for controlling new product development programs include predicting performance, allocating resources, reporting progress, and control of program execution.

PROGRESS REPORTING

The reporting of progress against the schedule provides information for management to use in evaluating the status of a project at any time. On complex product development projects, control is difficult without correct, current information.

Information on the progress of work originates with those who are actually doing the work. When a scheduled part of the work is completed, those who have done it (or their immediate supervisors) report this fact to the next higher level of management, and from there the report proceeds along the chain of management.

Information on progress and manpower and material utilization may also be used as input to an information processing system which prepares reports for different levels of management.

For proper progress reporting, managers at each level must be able to determine

1. Whether the current estimated time and cost for completing the entire project are realistic.
2. Whether the project is meeting the committed schedule and cost estimate and, if not, the extent of any difference.
3. Whether requirements for manpower and other resources have been planned realistically to minimize premium costs and idle time.
4. Whether those areas developing potential delays or cost overruns can be identified in time to permit corrective action.

5. How manpower and other resources can be shifted to expedite critical activities.
6. How manpower and other resources made available by changes in the project tasks can best be utilized.[2]

These progress reporting considerations for controlling new product development projects, manifested in modern systems techniques, are developed in Chapter 3 in the form of network analysis and are integrated into a corporate system for planning and control in Chapter 4.

BUDGETING

A budget is a financial plan of action for a program covering a definite period of time. Its purpose is to coordinate the activities of the various organizations involved in a project, aid management in securing control over different parts of the program, and find the most profitable course over which the efforts of the program may be directed. To achieve this end, a development budget reflects not only a plan, but also a standard by which the performance and accomplishments of managers involved in a development program can be measured.

The advantages and benefits of a budgetary system are manifold. In itself, a budget neither controls nor sets policies; it is a management tool which reflects policy. Its discipline helps develop a balanced program for the utilization of corporate resources, whether manpower, facilities, or finances. It helps management stabilize the use of its resources and thus prevents waste.

Since the budget is management's plan of action, it serves as a formal means of establishing corporate policy and advising various echelons of management what their financial goals and targets are.

The development of a budget for a new product is a complicated task. A budget is essentially an estimate of future costs broken down by cost categories. In order to prepare this estimate for a new product, a great deal of information must be accumulated and projected. The procedure used by a large, multimillion-dollar manufacturing

[2] *DOD and NASA Guide—PERT/Cost* (Washington, D.C.: Office of the Secretary of Defense/National Aeronautics and Space Administration, June 1962), pp. 1–2.

firm located in the Southwest will show one approach to developing a budget for a new industrial product for which initial research efforts have been completed.

First, a product projection study was initiated by the staff director of marketing aided by executives from sales, finance, manufacturing, and engineering. The study first required market research data to determine the sales potential of the new industrial product. Since the product had a potential application in many markets, each of the markets was analyzed in terms of the number of end products produced in the previous fiscal year. These end products were then identified as to whether they might (possible applications) or would not (negative applications) provide a market for the product under review. The number of end products with possible applications extended by the units of the new product developed its potential in terms of units and dollars for the five-year period under consideration. Also prepared were figures for the firm's historical sales and percentage participation in each of the potential markets. Projections were extended to possibilities of further market penetration based on price, quality, and sales coverage.

Through field study and customer contact, potential was verified by a study of competition, using a direct, competitive, or comparable method. To complete the program it was also necessary to make a detailed study of distribution methods and techniques not previously required to find out if the potential in a market might outstrip production capacity. At this point, the study projected a multimillion dollar increase in sales of 300 percent within five years.

Looking to production problems, the study proceeded from this point to project units and dollars in terms of styles and sizes—total potential as well as estimated participation by the firm. It provided the starting point for manufacturing projections. The analysis of the manufacturing aspects of the required expansion covered:

1. Equipment requirements and production capacity.
2. Equipment (selection and automation).
3. Manpower requirements.
4. Plant layout and plant location.
5. Manufacturing expense.
6. Cost reduction (materials and labor cost).
7. Detailed manufacturing problems to be resolved.

Following the bill of materials "explosion," units of the product were reduced to parts requirements in terms of present equipment capacity and projected requirements for machine capacity during each of the years under study. These capacity requirements were developed by total parts cost, machine and capital expenditures in amount and date cash is required. Summarized in terms of individual machines and dollars, a proposed capital investment of over $2 million became evident.

Based on the production requirements as indicated for the five-year period and the inventory of equipment required to effect this production, a manpower study was completed to determine the machines, shifts, and people required. Understandably, a plant layout study was also required. This study included plant location and activity relocation covering the usual items of freight rates, labor availability and labor rates, detail layout of manufacturing and service facilities, and total expenditures required. After the preparation of raw data, a detailed yearly manufacturing expense projection was prepared for the five-year period.

The point of departure for the marketing expense budget was the sales projection data. Preliminary work in reference to an overall expense figure—the amount that would be needed to sell a projected sales volume—was initiated. Using information on the sales-expense ratio at different sales volumes and the trend in this ratio as a guideline, the marketing expense budget was prepared.

With these data in hand, a projected profit and loss statement and estimated balance sheets for the five-year period were completed. This information was used in turn to develop working capital requirements and the base for the return-on-investment calculation.

At this firm the starting point for budgetary control is the form, Request for Development Authorization, which applies to any development expense or item beyond a determinable cost. These requests require the approval of the development and new products committee as well as the president, and they are prepared on the following basis:

- *Marketable product*—If an experimental product is to be manufactured and sold, the development authorization should cover all prospective expenditures for research, engineering, drawings, patterns, tools, and manufacturing of the experimental product, less a conservative carrying value.

- *Nonmarketable product*—When the development of an experimental product representing a new class, line, or type of standard product is contemplated and the experimental product is not placed on the market, the development authorization must include the working cost of developing and fabricating the product.

The reverse side of this request form covers additional data of distinct value to the development and new products committee in its consideration of the project. Included are these points:

1. Probable price obtainable.
2. Development time for first unit.
3. Probable sales, first year after development.
4. Probable sales per year thereafter.
5. Estimated commercial cost of subsequent units based on probable volume of sales as well as use of tools and equipment justified by such sales.
6. Extent to which field is now occupied or controlled by competitors.
7. Value of additional machinery required.
8. Value of permanent tools and fixtures required.

The development and new products committee, at its regular meeting during the final week of each quarter, passes on the development budget for the ensuing quarter. In establishing the overall amount of the development budget, the committee adheres generally, although not rigidly, to an amount determined as a percentage of the volume of orders booked.

Now that the planning and control requirements of product development programs have been explored, it is possible to review briefly recent management planning, control, and organizational approaches. These approaches not only satisfy the requirements just discussed but provide management with greater flexibility, better communications, improved planning action, and improved decision making. These techniques are network analysis and program management concepts, which are discussed briefly in the next chapter. Following an explanation of the fundamentals of these techniques, an integrated system for planning and controlling product development programs is presented.

3

Network Analysis and
Program Management Concepts

MANAGING A PRODUCT development program is a big job, and many devices must be employed to aid the manager in determining exactly what must be done, who should do it and when, where the program now stands, and what obstacles are to be faced and overcome in the future. This chapter is an introduction to and a description of a comparatively new management tool which is mainly a technique concerned with looking ahead and trying to anticipate trouble.

History of Network Analysis

Network analysis, also known as program evaluation and review technique (PERT), was developed in 1958 at the Navy Special Projects Office by a project team which studied the application of statistical and mathematical methods to the planning, evaluation, and control of research and development effort. The project team consisted of personnel from the U.S. Navy Special Projects Office; Booz, Allen & Hamilton Inc.; and Lockheed Missile Systems Division. The Navy first applied PERT to the development of the Polaris missile program. Within a few years the technique had found application in certain areas of the Air Force, Army, and special agencies of the government as well as in private industry.

WHAT IS NETWORK ANALYSIS?

Network analysis is a procedure which serves as a management control tool for defining and integrating what must be done to accomplish program objectives on time. At the present time, this evaluation is limited to the time dimension; that is, it generally assumes resources will be applied as required to meet a time schedule. Accordingly, this procedure is best adapted to development programs where priority and resources do not continually vary. This technique aids the decision maker but does not make decisions for him. It can be used as a statistical technique that quantifies knowledge about the uncertainties faced in those activities that contribute to meeting a predetermined time schedule. It is particularly helpful when there are many activities with complex interrelationships, when there are many different people or groups concerned, and when good information flow is important as an aid to decision making and communication. It facilitates the economic control of time, manpower, materials, and money.

The very process of analyzing the uncertainties involved in certain activities focuses management attention on the critical areas where new product decisions must be made as to the corrective actions necessary to maintain a schedule. The analysis of outputs permits evaluation of the trade-offs in time and the redistribution of resources that may improve the chances of meeting time schedules.

When the product development project network goes into operation, there is a need to clarify responsibilities, issue working schedules, monitor progress, update the project situation, and provide management with sufficient information for decision making. Networks are not a panacea, nor are they necessarily a replacement for existing techniques.

Basic PERT—Events

Exhibit 16 shows a small sample network which is taken from a larger operating network used for a new product launch. *Networks* of events and activities are the basic elements of the procedure. A network is a graphic presentation of the individual events, activities, and interrelationships of a one-time project. It is, in effect, a road map of planning work which shows the proper sequence of all steps of the job. This sample network is representative of the lowest level of detail found in operating networks for typical consumer products development programs. This is the level at which the design and development work is actually carried out, and the activities on the network represent the "inherent" or "intrinsic" size of tasks (in weeks in this exhibit). The network, therefore, also represents the amount of detail required by operating-level supervision, if not by higher management.

The circles (they can be ellipses or squares) on the network are called events. *Events*, as shown on the chart, are meaningful specific accomplishments, either physical or intellectual, that do not consume time or resources. They may be such accomplishments as program go-ahead, start design, complete design, start fabrication, complete fabrication, order parts, or receive parts. For instance, Event 1, deal approved, would represent the receipt of approval of the particular sales promotion deal in accordance with an established format and procedure; Event 9, start manufacturing display, would represent the receipt of plates and approval of display proofs needed to start manufacturing the display material.

Event 1 is called the *starting event* and Event 12 the *terminating* or ending event for this particular network. If the network in Exhibit 16 is considered a subnetwork (part of a larger network), Events 1 and 12 might be called *milestone events*. If this network is considered to be one of a group of networks, Event 12 might be called an interface event. In this case, the event would occur in another network with the same description and event numbers.

Activities

Activities are defined as any jobs or work elements which occupy time and consume resources. An event is separated from other events

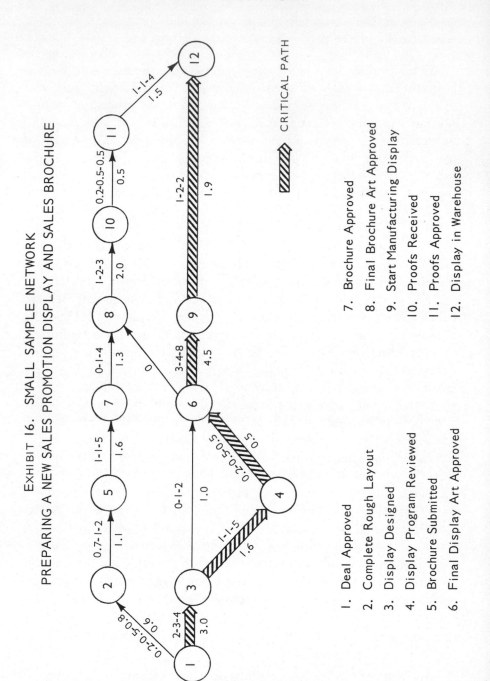

EXHIBIT 16. SMALL SAMPLE NETWORK
PREPARING A NEW SALES PROMOTION DISPLAY AND SALES BROCHURE

CRITICAL PATH

1. Deal Approved
2. Complete Rough Layout
3. Display Designed
4. Display Program Reviewed
5. Brochure Submitted
6. Final Display Art Approved

7. Brochure Approved
8. Final Brochure Art Approved
9. Start Manufacturing Display
10. Proofs Received
11. Proofs Approved
12. Display in Warehouse

by activities. On a network this is usually shown by an arrow that connects the events and indicates the beginning and ending events. An activity is defined by its *predecessor and successor* event numbers. An activity represents elapsed time, usually stated in 7 day calendar weeks with an assumed 5-day, 40-hour workweek. Activities carrying a time estimate which is not zero also represent the *expenditure of resources*, usually in terms of manpower and material. An exception to this is an activity which does not represent an expenditure of resources; this is the so-called *dummy* or *zero-time* activity. An example of a dummy activity is shown between Events 6 and 8 in Exhibit 16. This dummy activity is used to indicate a constraint not requiring resources; in this particular network, it indicates that final brochure art can be approved after final display art is approved, but not until then.

NETWORK LOGIC

There are five important ground rules connected with the handling of events and activities on a network. These ground rules, commonly recognized by PERT practitioners, must be followed in order to maintain the correct topology of the network.

Ground Rule 1. Each activity must have a predecessor and successor event. Similarly, each event must have a preceding and succeeding activity, with the exception of starting and terminating events. However, an event may have *more than one* preceding and succeeding activity.

Ground Rule 2. No activity may start until its predecessor event is completed; in turn, no event may be considered complete until all activities leading into it have been completed. This is the key topological ground rule of the networking technique.

Ground Rule 3. There are cases in network analysis where two or more activities can exist, in effect, between any one pair of predecessor and successor events, as shown on the left-hand portion of Exhibit 17. This situation sometimes occurs where technical uncertainty is involved in one of the activities and a "back-up" or "redundant" activity is added. As shown in Exhibit 17, the existence of two activities between any one pair of events would produce an

EXHIBIT 17.   GROUND RULE 3—HANDLING OF PARALLEL ACTIVITIES

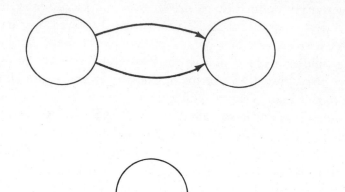

ambiguity, since both activities would have the same predecessor and successor event number and description. The preferred method of handling the situation, which involves the introduction of a dummy activity, appears in the right-hand portion of Exhibit 17.

Ground Rule 4. There is one other situation where a dummy activity is introduced; this is usually referred to as the *dependent and independent activity* situation. In Exhibit 18(a), Activities C and D are shown as being *dependent* upon the completion of Activities A and B. It may be, however, that Activity D is *independent* of the completion of Activity A, while C is not. In this case, the preferred method of handling is shown in Exhibit 18(b). A somewhat similar situation can occur when the results of two independent activities are to be merged into a single follow-up activity as shown in Exhibit 18(c). The preferred version of handling this situation is shown in Exhibit 18(d).

Ground Rule 5. The last topological ground rule for network

EXHIBIT 18. GROUND RULE 4—ILLUSTRATION

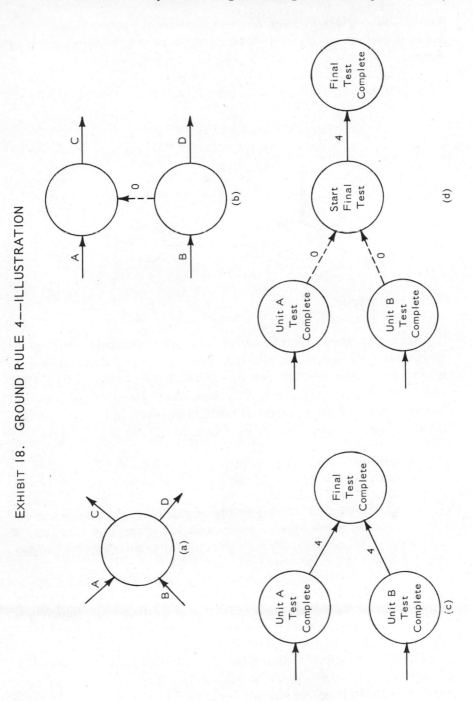

construction refers to looping. No given event can be followed by an activity path which leads back to the same event. An example of looping is shown in Exhibit 19.

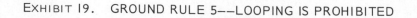

EXHIBIT 19.   GROUND RULE 5—LOOPING IS PROHIBITED

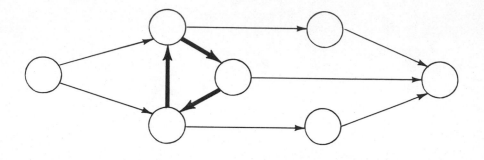

Time Estimating

After a *network configuration* has been established—in other words, after all events and activities have been identified and drawn up in accordance with the previous ground rules—*elapsed-time estimates* are made for each activity. In the CPM technique only a single-activity elapsed-time estimate is made. However, the PERT technique permits three time estimates of an activity:

1. *Optimistic time.* This is the time which would be required if everything proceeded ideally; it has no more than 1 chance in 100 of being realized.
2. *Pessimistic time.* Barring totally uncontrollable situations such as fires and floods, this is the time that would be required if everything which could logically go wrong does go wrong; it also has only 1 chance in 100 of being realized.
3. *Most likely time.* This is the time which the estimator really thinks will be required for the job. It is also the time that the activity would take most often if it could be repeated numerous times under exactly the same conditions.

These three estimates should be made by the people most familiar with the activity; they cannot be arbitrarily selected by planners who may then attempt to rig the network so that it will coincide with the scheduled completion date. Rigging can be attempted on a simplified network and where long periods of time are involved, but it cannot be carried on indefinitely. Sooner or later the network will become realistic, especially as scheduled dates are approached.

It must also be remembered that these estimates of activity are made one at a time without regard to adjacent activities because the intent is to get a realistic appraisal of a task to be done. *A task is an activity.*

Estimates are always expressed in weeks or fractions thereof without regard to calendar dates, because it is easy to transpose time in weeks to a calendar date. This date can be dependent upon the starting date or upon any other date programmed into the network.

NETWORK CALCULATIONS

The planner first calculates the activity time for each activity by converting the three time estimates to a single calculated time. Exhibit 20 shows these calculated activity times. This time is computed as follows:

$$t_e = \text{calculated activity time} = \frac{a + 4m + b}{6}.$$

In this equation, a is the optimistic time, b the pessimistic time, and m the most likely time.

The mathematics of this equation are discussed in the appendix. It is apparent, however, that the distribution of the three time estimates may vary in many ways on either side of the estimated most likely time. The calculated activity time obtained from the equation gives an estimated mean for the range of distributions to be encountered.

Cumulative event-expected time—T_E. The next step involves calculating the event-expected time for each event by adding the calculated activity time (t_e) from the initial event to each subsequent event. This is done for every possible path of events leading to the end event. T_E for any event is the *longest path leading to that event;* the resulting T_E value then represents the *earliest time* that the event can be completed.

EXHIBIT 20.   EXHIBIT 16 WITH T_E AND T_L CALCULATIONS

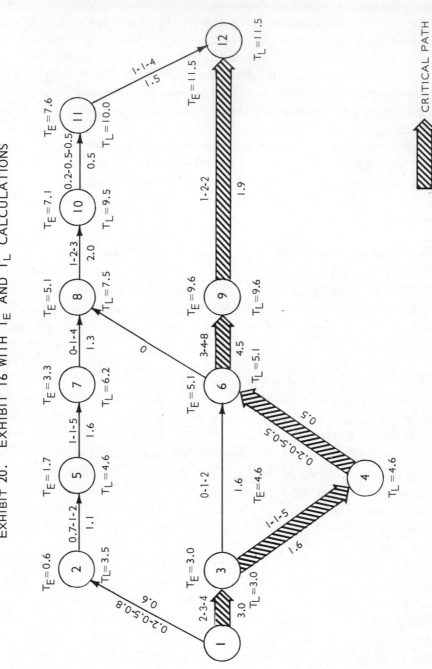

CRITICAL PATH

This can be verified from Exhibit 20, which represents Exhibit 16 with individual T_E calculations above each event. Leading into Event 6 there are two possible paths, one with a T_E value of 3.0 + 1.6, or 4.6, and the other with a T_E value of 4.6 + 0.5, or 5.1. The T_E of 5.1, being the larger of the two figures and representing the longest path leading into Event 6, is the dominant one. The same situation exists at Event 12, where it can be verified that the correct T_E is 11.5 coming in from Event 9, rather than 9.1 coming in from Event 11. By calculating the T_E's for every event, which involves starting at the beginning of the network and examining all paths leading into any one event, the "forward pass" through the network is completed.

Latest allowable time—T_L. The next step involves determining the latest time at which an event can be completed and still not disturb the completion time of the terminating or end event of the network. We label this the latest allowable time, T_L, for an event. The latest allowable time is calculated conversely to T_E. We "anchor" the network on 11.5 weeks and make a "backward pass" through the network (see Exhibit 20). At Event 6, the longest *backward path* from End Event 12 leads through Events 9 and 6 and produces a T_L equal to 11.5 − 1.9 − 4.5, or 5.1. The other path leading back to Event 6 is through Events 11, 10, and 8 and is equal to 11.5 − 1.5 − 0.5 − 2.0 − 0, or 7.5. It will be noted that the *smaller* figure of 5.1 is chosen for T_L, since it represents the *longest* backward path. This process is continued through each path, always retaining the smaller T_L.

Slack—Slack is defined as the amount of time that an event time can be allowed to slip without changing the completion time of the final event. This can be computed by subtracting T_E from T_L for each activity.

$$\text{Slack} = T_L - T_E.$$

THE CRITICAL PATH

Exhibit 20 shows the *critical path* of events through the network. *It is the longest path through the network. Any slippage along this critical path will produce a slippage in the end event.* The diagram also includes the calculated activity times between events which were obtained from the three time estimates previously discussed.

According to the output data, it will take at least 11.5 weeks to complete the sales promotion display and sales brochure, and the events on the critical path are 1 through 3 through 4 through 6 through 9 to 12. All other events will have some degree of slack, which allows the planner to reallocate resources to improve the situation on the critical path, that is, to focus attention on the events and activities that will most improve the completion time of the end event.

Criticalness is measured in times of negative, zero, or positive slack. Positive slack indicates an ahead-of-schedule condition, negative slack indicates a behind-schedule condition, and zero slack indicates an on-schedule condition with a probability of 0.5. Negative slack occurs when the total activity time along a path is greater than the time available to meet the program requirements.

After a network is completed, the required time as well as the critical path can be examined in detail. It now becomes permissible to see what would happen if certain times were changed. This simulation produces alternate courses of action and a choice of decisions.

Other Third-Generation Techniques and Extensions of PERT

More detailed third-generation planning and control techniques exist, but they are essentially beyond the scope of this book. However, the relationship of PERT to systems engineering, PERT/cost, and PERT/reliability will be outlined to show what these extensions are and how they relate to the problems of planning and control of product development activities.

PERT/cost, an extension of the basic PERT technique, utilizes a common framework for planning the schedule and cost of a program. As in the PERT system, the program is first defined and then, through a work breakdown structure, is broken down into end-item subdivisions and then into work packages. A work package is a unit of work required to complete a specific job—such as a report, a design, a plan, a piece of equipment, or a service—which is within the responsibility of one operating unit in an organization. The work packages are then represented by one or more activities on a conventional PERT network to identify the interdependencies in the program and the sequence in which the work will be performed.

After the network has been prepared and the schedule for the program has been established, the responsible operating and management personnel develop cost estimates for each work package, basing the costs on the manpower and other resources required to perform the program on schedule. These estimates are made by first determining the manpower, material, and other resources required to perform each work package. The resource estimates are then converted to dollars to determine the direct cost of each package. Indirect costs are added to work packages where such accumulation is possible by existing accounting procedure or as required by contracts. All other indirect costs are prorated at the summary level of the program on the basis of total program indirect cost already accumulated or assigned.

Separate cost estimates are not, as a rule, necessary for each activity in a work package, since they can result in excessive details and unrealistic accounting effort.

The cost estimate for a work package is affected by both the elapsed time required to perform the work package and the calendar period during which the work package is scheduled to occur. The latest schedule status is considered in preparing cost estimates for work packages and in planning the allocation of resources. Operating and management personnel analyze the estimates to eliminate unnecessary manpower costs and premium payments for materials and services.

For example, monthly manpower requirements are totaled by skill and then examined to minimize the unnecessary overtime and hiring caused by manpower peaks followed by layoffs. This manpower smoothing is accomplished by rescheduling slack activities to periods when the skills are not required by critical activities. Rescheduling slack activities can also eliminate or reduce premium payments for materials and services.

Periodic comparisons are made of the actual costs incurred for each work package with their current estimates. This comparison establishes the cost status of the program and identifies any incurred cost overruns. Estimates of the cost of completing work not yet performed are also obtained in order to predict future cost overruns and to identify difficulties in the performance of critical work packages early enough to take constructive management action.

The level of detail to which it is desirable to apply PERT/cost is largely a matter of judgment; it varies from program to program, from one part of a program to another, and from the proposal preparation stage to the execution stage of the same project.

PERT/reliability is a third-generation extension of the basic PERT technique which relates the extent of end-item reliability (the degree to which a product can be depended upon to perform what is expected or required) to a schedule so that a composite evaluation of product reliability is continuously determined as the program progresses.

Two general approaches toward greater reliability have been adopted. The first approach attempts to put a numerical value on the expected operational reliability of the end item: By measurement or test, a number indicates how many times out of how many trials an item will perform as specified. This simple ratio is a measure of reliability.

The second approach tries to increase reliability by monitoring the documentation required as a part of good engineering practice. Under this method, the development plan is monitored to see that there is compliance with the basic design, the specifications, reliability-test procedures, acceptance test procedures, and so forth. Proper compliance with these reliability-event documents should result in a more reliable product. The ratio of compliance is known as the reliability-maturity index (RMI). In the RMI extension to PERT, two ratings are made for each reliability event—the technical quality evaluation (TQE) and schedule compliance evaluation (SCE). The average of these two ratings provides the reliability-maturity index (RMI).

The technical quality evaluation is an independent audit of the reliability-event documents. It is a report that evaluates an activity that has culminated in a reliability event such as design specifications, design review, qualification specifications, qualification test, acceptance specifications, or acceptance test. An arithmetical process yields a number between 0 and 100 which is the TQE of the activity.

Schedule compliance evaluation provides the planning, scheduling, reporting, and monitoring functions of RMI. Two different SCE rating values are calculated for each assembly:

1. A relative composite rating is derived by totaling the actual number of reliability-event documents completed as of a report's date and dividing by the number of reliability-event documents scheduled to have been completed *by that date.*
2. A cumulative composite rating is derived by totaling the actual number of reliability-event documents completed as of a report's date and dividing by the number of reliability-events documents scheduled *for the total program.*

Systems engineering. This is a recently recognized specialization which evolved from the large and complex weapon-system developments of the 1950's. The systems engineer is concerned with examining the *best possible ways* of achieving the primary goals of a program or the mission effectiveness of a system by utilizing existing or within-the-state-of-the-art technology. Then he is concerned with optimizing or making the best possible trade-offs between performance factors (such as speed, cycle time, maintainability, and reliability) against time and cost factors. Following this, he must make explicit recommendations for a system which will have an acceptable cost-effectiveness ratio.

These systems analysis requirements are difficult, but the systems engineer has an even more complex task in defining the effectiveness or value of a system. The concept of effectiveness or value is of interest to the businessman who is launching a new product and is concerned about how the product will fare in the marketplace, particularly about how it will stand up against competitive new product developments. Exhibit 21 graphically indicates this concept of value. The curve shows that value is at a low or even negative figure during the early development period when the product, if it were introduced, would be too advanced in character to be marketable.

The reason for the negative figure is the investment in development costs with no recovery from sales. Exhibit 21 shows that, in later stages of the development program, there is a peaking of the value or acceptability of the product after which value declines with the passage of time. It is the declining portion of the value curve that is concerned with the concept of a penalty cost—the cost of not bringing a product onto the market at the earliest possible time. The systems engineer is concerned with the increasing penalty cost to a firm for not having a new product developed in time to meet competitive activity. It is, however, extremely difficult to quantify such

EXHIBIT 21.   VALUE OF DEVELOPMENT PROGRAM RESULTS

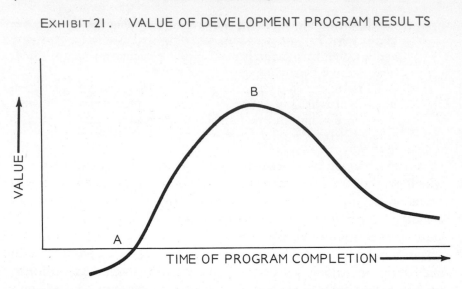

a value or effectiveness curve for a new product development program.

Nevertheless, it is the job of systems engineering to choose, if not an optimum, at least a sharply reduced number of system configurations out of all the possibilities that exist. When this is done, it is possible to establish a product breakdown with an associated set of end-item performance requirements. These results of systems engineering are necessary to establish the product-oriented end-item subdivisions of the work breakdown structure.

INTRODUCTION TO PROGRAM MANAGEMENT

The project management concept has emerged over a period of years out of the unique requirements of the U.S. defense industry. New management techniques were needed that could be applied across organizational lines to accomplish a specific undertaking, such as developing a ballistic missile system. Although the techniques were developed to meet the needs of the defense industry, many other industries have adopted the concepts and have applied them to their own problems.

Much of product development activity is carried out in the form of projects. Cutting through the morass of routine, day-to-day activities, the task force and the crash program have become the order of the day. This stream of projects requires, each with its own problems and peculiarities, that an individual be appointed project manager, with the responsibility for keeping abreast of all the company's work on that project. Project (or program) management, therefore, is a general management activity and includes such functions as planning, organizing, motivating, integrating, directing, and controlling efforts to obtain a specific goal. Typically, then, a project organization is responsible for completing an assigned objective on schedule, within cost and profit goals, and in accord with established standards. The objective usually requires special management attention and emphasis for a long period of time.

Within the framework of product development activities, the need for program management may be evident. With many projects on hand, the product development manager may find it extremely difficult to keep up with the many projects and functional efforts demanding his attention. Top management then may find it advantageous to make one individual responsible for each of the projects and let him continue in that role for the life of the project.

CHARACTERISTICS OF PROGRAM MANAGEMENT

Program management has several characteristics that do not exist in traditional management:

1. A project task is *finite* in duration. It has a definite end point at which the project is complete: The product is in market testing; the house is built and ready for occupancy; the sales brochure is printed and in the warehouse—all goals have been achieved, and the "specs" have been met.
2. Project management is concerned with an *identifiable end item or product*. A project should be definable in terms of a specific goal.
3. A project is *homogeneous*. The individual activities can be classified as belonging to a specific project. This implies that projects are entities and have an edge, a boundary, that distinguishes them from their institutional environment. More precisely, using a

PERT network diagram as an example, this means that a project has a greater density of dependency, *within* itself, than exists between it and its surroundings. In fact, this is how one can approximate the boundary of a project. It is the zone where there are relatively few activities leading outward, where there seems to be a natural line of perforation.

4. A project is *complex*. It requires a fairly involved mixture of serial and parallel work tasks or activities and uses a significant mixture of human skills, resources, materials, and facilities. Since many of the people involved in a project are professional and creative personnel outside the project manager's line authority, he must use management techniques different from those used in the traditional superior-subordinate relationships. He must temper the traditional processes with motivation and persuasion. In addition, leading professionals often require that the rationale of the effort be stated so that they can understand more thoroughly and contribute more meaningfully.

5. Project management requires that functional lines (parent company) and organizational lines (outside organizations) be crossed to accomplish project activities. Project management is more concerned with the flow of work in horizontal and diagonal relationships than with vertical scalar chains of authority. (See Exhibit 22.) But project management cannot exist alone. When project management techniques are introduced, two complementary organizations will exist in the company: (*a*) the traditional pyramid organization and (*b*) the project organization. In this organizational arrangement, each project manager is concerned with a finite project to be developed and produced in terms of desired cost, schedule, and performance characteristics. The functional managers and the project manager share the responsibility and authority for the project activities as follows.

The project manager

1. Unifies the project affairs so that top management and the ultimate consumer or customer are satisfied.
2. Establishes the funding, scheduling, and performance standards for the project.
3. Acts as the focal point for customer contact in the company.
4. Resolves any conflict that threatens to disrupt the project activities.

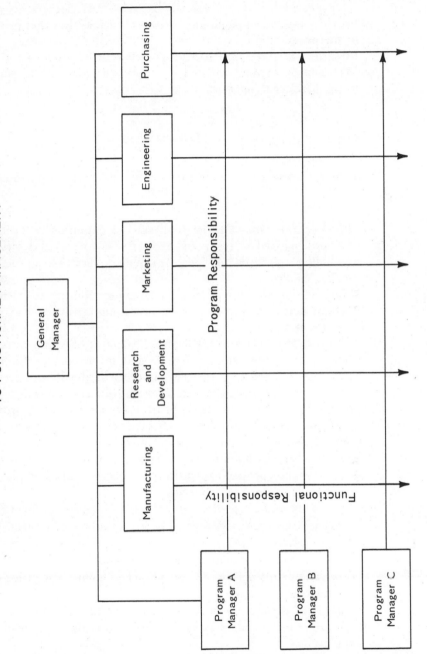

EXHIBIT 22. MATRIX ORGANIZATION—RELATIONSHIP OF PROGRAM MANAGEMENT TO FUNCTIONAL MANAGEMENT

The functional manager

1. Provides functional facilitation to this as well as the other projects in the organization.
2. Prescribes *how* the day-to-day projects will be supported.
3. Maintains an existing capability in terms of the state of the art in the particular function.

RESPONSIBILITIES OF PROGRAM MANAGEMENT

To be able to wield total control, a project organization must be responsible for:

1. *Product definition*—Define or direct the definition of products to be developed in terms of hardware, software, and services, including standards for performance, quality, reliability, and maintainability.
2. *Task and funds control*—Assign tasks and allocate funds to all groups performing the tasks or procuring hardware and services for the project.
3. *Make-or-buy decisions*—Coordinate analyses of company capabilities, capacities, and efficiencies and make final decisions on whether the company supplies or buys hardware and services for the project. Participate in selection of major sources.
4. *Scheduling*—Develop master project schedules and coordinate schedule requirements with affected company organizations, associate subcontractors, and customers.
5. *Project status*—Establish status-reporting systems and continuously monitor project expenditures, schedules, task completions, cost to complete, and deliveries.
6. *Identification and solution of problems*—Identify problems significant to project success and initiate action to solve them.
7. *Project change control*—Approve and exercise control over all project changes, including design changes.
8. *Associate or subcontractor control*—Have control of major subcontractors (advertising agency, outside designers, vendors, and others) involved in team arrangements on major tasks.
9. *Customer and public relations*—Serve as the outside contact for the project.

10. *Market potentials*—Maintain awareness of customer attitudes, customer desires, and any other factors which could affect the project. Develop plans for logical follow-up action, potential or new applications, or new versions of the potential product or services.*

Program Management—A New Organizational Concept

Establishing a project environment requires a new organizational structure which reflects major work relationships rather than the traditional work alignments. This organizational structure is normally composed of four major elements.

1. *Functional support.* In a manufacturing organization, the technological base would be supplied by three groups providing for production, marketing, and finance. Functional support not only supports all projects in the organization, but advances the short-range state of the art in a particular discipline.

2. *Project management.* This consists of a set of managers each acting as a *unifying agent* for a particular project in respect to the current resources of time, funds, materials, people, and technology.

3. *Routine administration.* The accommodating services providing for mission-related activities include the centralized activities required to keep score on the business as a whole, as well as the routine administration and accounting of funds, people, materials, and ideas. Examples are the personnel function and the accounting function.

4. *Research and development/long-range planning.* These activities advance the *strategic* state of the art in the functional areas of interest to the company and develop a system of plans for the company's future. This group is less concerned with accomplishing current work than with obtaining future work and finding new uses for existing resources; consequently, the work is more conceptual and abstract than that of other elements.

The organization for project management should include some type of formalized structure for efficient collective action. The groups

* C. J. Middleton, "How to Set Up a Project Organization," *Harvard Business Review*, March/April 1967, p. 75.

required to work on the project are not reflected in a neat pyramidal organization, but are concentrated around the project as the need arises.

Project authority is the total influence that the project manager exercises over the schedule, cost, and technical considerations of the project. He should have broad authority over all elements of the project. Authority of the project manager flows horizontally, diagonally, and vertically. A significant portion of his authority depends on his ability to resolve conflicts, to build alliances and reciprocity, and to maintain the integrity of the project team.

4

A Planning and Control System for Product Development Programs

NEW PRODUCT PLANNING and development programs have many characteristics in common with defense-system programs. Weapons-system-oriented industries faced with complex, special-purpose programs have utilized management science and operations research techniques to cope with the time, cost, and performance characteristics unique to those programs. It is now possible to utilize these modern systems techniques in order to develop a planning and control system specifically designed for product development programs.

The tangible and intangible benefits to be achieved from an effective planning and control system are as follows:

1. A basic improvement in planning, which allows for better decision making prior to entering upon new programs.
2. A greatly improved ability to control programs against original objectives.

3. The possibility of executing complex development programs within the original estimates of time and cost.
4. The potential for actual cost savings, increases in efficiency, and improvement in profits.
5. Effective communication among persons working toward a common goal.
6. The opportunity for trade-offs between time, cost, and performance criteria.

The properties of such a system specifically designed for the problems of new product development include:

1. Clearly defined objectives of each program.
2. Predictive capabilities.
3. Integration in all organizations at all levels of management.
4. All interdependencies shown.
5. All tasks and activities shown.
6. Resource allocation capabilities.
7. Consideration of uncertainty and risk.
8. Adaptiveness to program management requirements.
9. Availability of alternative courses of action.
10. Risk analysis capabilities.
11. Simulation capabilities.
12. Ease of manipulation and control.
13. Hierarchy of details possible.
14. Easily obtained critical aspects of program.
15. Responsiveness to program changes.
16. Automatic updating capabilities.
17. Automatic replanning features.
18. Immediate status information with rapid turnaround time.
19. Easy comprehension at all levels of management.

MANAGEMENT OF A PROGRAM UNDER AN INTEGRATED SYSTEM

In order to utilize the disciplines of network analysis and program management to meet the planning and control requirements of product development programs, an integrated system is required. Experience has indicated the usefulness of these approaches as planning, evaluation, and control techniques for development projects. The product development planning and control system presented here incorporates the productive knowledge and experience that has been gained through these efforts.

By using the following guideline system design, performing departments and organizations involved in product development activities will create a basis for the routine flow of appropriate information required by higher levels of management and also will make available the more detailed back-up information which may be needed on an exception basis.

This discussion is intended as a guide for implementation and for a systematic development of a product development planning and control system (PDPCS). The system serves not only the higher-level management requirements of corporate top management but also the project planning and control requirements of operating organizations. The objective is to provide the information for better planning and control of time and cost in product development projects.

PREPARATION, SUPERVISION, AND APPROVAL

It is important, when establishing a product planning system within a company, to distinguish between the overall planning responsibility at the top management level and the interfunctional and functional planning responsibility at lower levels of management. It is quite clear that incompleteness of understanding or performance at the corporate or summary levels of a new product system has a direct effect on performance at detailed functional levels. Further, correction of problems at these levels is of prime value to system success both because of the multiplier effect and because guidelines at this level are more universal.

Top management planning responsibilities concern the company as a whole. They deal with those issues which affect the company's future shape and purpose, its guiding policies, and its general organization. Stated in terms of product planning, they focus on the development of strategies designed to achieve overall company objectives (for example, profit, growth, and diversification) through planned sequential introduction of new or revised products. Interfunctional planning involves several management functions in a closely coordinated single plan of action; for example, product planning and manpower planning. They cut across functional lines toward specified objectives which require the allocation of resources—manpower, money, and the rest—over some appreciable period of time. It is this kind of planning that we are concerned with here. Functional planning is the generally accepted planning performed by each management function—manufacturing, marketing, engineering, and so on.

Within the framework of a product planning system, most planners break a new products program into a six-stage pattern in order to manage and control the process—exploration, screening, business analysis, development, testing, and commercialization. The basic idea for stages of effort was first developed to correct the general looseness of planning in this area of new product projects, especially a concern that there were no intermediate points in a project and that, once started, a project developed a momentum that carried it along. This problem was resolved by the adoption of stages of activity requiring management go/no-go decisions between stages.

Some companies carried this work further; they developed specific outlines of what each functional organization should do stage by stage and established criteria for go/no-go review at the end of each major development stage. In some cases, the procedures at the end of each stage called for concurrence and comments by company staff groups on those elements of the plan for which they have functional responsibility, such as financial projections, production costs or implications, and capital budget requirements.

For top-level planning of new products, the strategic implications of products selected for development and subsequent launch can be considered at two levels, each related ultimately to cost and risk. At the first strategic level are those new or revised products selected from products which have already been tried in test markets. At the second strategic level are those potential new products brought to test market by a process that provides for comprehensive go/no-go review at the end of each major development stage, thereby avoiding unnecessary development expense for the projects with limited chance of test market success. At the first level are products whose chances of success are fairly well known; at the second level, products whose continuous review avoids unnecessary expense and insures the evaluation of risk.

A new product development program generally begins when top management approves a product idea for development. Project management effort is generally not concerned with the development of a marketing plan including idea search, concept development, or preliminary economic analysis—all of which precede development go-ahead.

By the time a development go decision is made, the preliminary exploration, screening, and business analysis stages have been completed. These stages are most often performed by corporate planning, marketing, or research executives and do not involve the complex coordination that later stages require. In some cases, the executive who performs the preliminary analysis may prepare initial summary or skeleton networks in order to determine rough lead times, project costs, and risks. This work contributes to the analysis and aids in obtaining the development go decision. As soon as possible after this decision is made, a project manager should be selected and made responsible for guiding the project to completion within the framework of the PDPCS.

Certain individuals selected from departments involved in the product development project have the responsibility for

1. Developing the events and activities their organization will contribute into the integrated project network.
2. Coordinating the efforts of their department as they apply to the product development project.
3. Executing their phase of the activities on the network.
4. Reporting status and progress information as required.

PROGRAM COORDINATION

The project manager is basically responsible for overall project coordination. His functions are, as they relate to the system, to

1. Coordinate and authorize the activities of the project team.
2. Develop the project definition.
3. Coordinate the development of a project network.
4. Review and approve project schedules.
5. Develop a project replan as required.

Project scheduling is also the responsibility of the project manager. He may have a staff assigned to assist him with scheduling, or there may be an existing scheduling staff within the company on which he can draw for aid. No matter where the scheduling staff reports, it acts as an agent of the project manager for the scheduling of and progress monitoring on his project.

The scheduling function serves not only the project manager, but also the company management and the personnel responsible for the work on the project. This central staff group should be composed of network analysts who have a thorough background in computer technology, engineering, and planning disciplines in addition to being familiar with company organizations and operations. Individuals from this group should train executives in the system, aid program managers in planning, and handle the details of networking, analysis, and computer liaison. This approach has been used successfully in such companies as National Dairy Products Corp., Dow Chemical Co., Texas Instruments Incorporated, Upjohn Co., Lever Brothers Co., U.S. Industrial Chemicals Co., Carborundum Co., and Colgate-Palmolive Co., and, of course, in the defense industries.

REPORTING SYSTEM REQUIREMENTS

Project schedules and progress reports are required at different levels of management. The reports include different levels of detail, depending on the level of management to which they are submitted. They indicate the project schedule, compare progress on parts of the project with the schedule, and compare actual resources utilization with what was scheduled. The parts of the project which may deviate from the schedule are closely monitored by the project manager and his management, especially if a delay in any one of them may delay the entire project.

Progress reporting may be made daily in an informal way, or it may be made less frequently. Progress may be reported more frequently on those parts of the project which are critical to timely completion of the project than on noncritical parts.

Information on progress and resource utilization may also be used as input to an information processing system which prepares reports for different levels of management. These reports may be prepared by the scheduling group or by a computer system. Many computer programs are available in almost infinite variety for PERT projects of all types. All computer manufacturers have programs available and can be contacted for further information.

EXECUTION OF A PROGRAM UNDER AN INTEGRATED SYSTEM

The PDPCS is an operating system which integrates network analysis, program management, and management information and reporting system techniques specifically designed for product development programs. (See Exhibit 23.)* The major aspects of the system will be described in operating sequence. Because of its feedback characteristic, the system is represented as a cycle with two components— the planning cycle and the control cycle.

As shown in Exhibit 23, the planning cycle should include ten steps:

1. Develop the project organization.
2. Implement system training.
3. Prepare the project definition.
4. Establish a project work breakdown structure.
5. Construct the networks.
6. Estimate activity times.
7. Apply network checklists and review.
8. Review the preliminary schedule.
9. Review and revise the plan.
10. Develop the final plan.

Also shown in Exhibit 23 are the nine steps in the control cycle:

1. Approve the plan and schedule.
2. Authorize work.
3. Distribute approved outputs.
4. Update the plan.
5. Prepare status reports.
6. Evaluate project status.
7. Recommend alternative courses of action.
8. Revise the plan and schedules.
9. Prepare higher management reports.

* The system was developed and implemented by the author at Lever Brothers Company in New York. The system is described briefly in an article by the author that appeared in the November 1968 issue of *The Systems and Procedures Journal.*

EXHIBIT 23.   PRODUCT DEVELOPMENT PLANNING AND CONTROL SYSTEM CYCLE

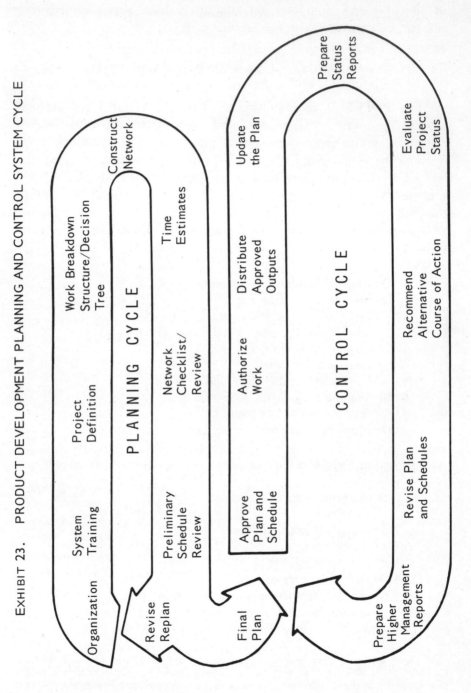

In order to show how this integrated management system is used in a product development project, let us consider an authentic application in a major consumer products manufacturing company. Although, for understandable reasons, certain elements have been purposely disguised, the validity of the approach is not altered.

For a number of years, the research and development group had been dabbling with an idea for a new consumer product in the cosmetic field that represented a significant breakthrough in terms of a viable, marketable concept. Suddenly, research efforts were accelerated when what appeared to be a workable formula was obtained. Top management, alerted by this progress, authorized additional marketing analysis to determine if the product represented a worthwhile business opportunity. When this was shown to be the case, a marketing manager was appointed to be responsible for the product.

Further analysis revealed that a recent innovation in the packaging field would be ideal for the packaging of this product. In fact, when this packaging approach was brought to the attention of the president, he indicated a strong preference for the new material. Preliminary testing by the research group on the compatibility of the product formulation with the new packaging material revealed a great number of problems that promised to delay the new product project. At this point, it was decided to develop a program plan for the project, and the network analysis staff was contacted.

Key executives involved in the project were requested to attend a meeting with the network analyst selected to monitor the project. At this meeting, the product development planning and control system was explained and individual responsibilities were assigned in developing a project definition. While developing the project definition at a second meeting, the packaging development lead-time problems were discussed. The network analyst, in attempting to determine the implications of these problems, used decision tree methodology to structure the alternatives, consequences, and risks involved in each of the proposed research approaches. This analysis showed that there were some twenty possible outcomes, but only three were feasible within the time and cost constraints of the program, and none of these three was favorable to the new packaging material that was of such interest to the president. In light of this new information, the marketing manager made the decision to drop the new packaging material from immediate consideration, but to continue development efforts for possible use in the future.

At this point, a work breakdown structure was prepared by the network analyst and submitted to key executives in the program for approval. Two network meetings were then scheduled; the first attended by the marketing group and executives from the advertising agency, sales, sales promotion, packaging development, packaging design, and market research, along with the network analyst. At this meeting a network was developed that extended to test market launch. The second meeting was attended by executives from the operations groups (including manufacturing, research and development, packaging design, purchasing, and engineering) and the network analyst. At this meeting the development tasks of operations executives were detailed and linked into the network developed at the previous meeting, with all interfaces depicted.

The result of these meetings was an initial plan for the program, done in a conservative and risk-free way, that showed all the events, activities, and interfaces in the development program up to test market launch. Time estimates were then added to the network. At this point, the network was checked by the analyst for all required activities. Since the company had a computer program for PERT, the network was then coded into computer format, cards were punched, and the network deck was run on the computer for the initial schedule. When run, the schedule showed a two-and-one-half-year lead time to test market launch, a time period far in excess of the requirements of top management. Obviously, replanning was necessary. It was also clear to see that, unless detailed network planning was attempted, the project would have unusual difficulty and that a no-risk program was unfeasible.

An analysis of the critical path and other limiting paths in the network showed program areas where time could be reduced. Three basic approaches were taken. In the first, certain portions of the work were eliminated. For example, research reports on findings were not required for decision making; the results could be telephoned and the decisions could be made, with the report following afterward for evaluation.

The second method was to make parallel those activities which normally would occur in series. For example, purchase orders for packaging material were to be released before packaging design was complete in order to allow vendors to purchase their raw materials early. This approach was considered expensive because of the additional risks that had to be taken.

The third method used was the application of additional resources —more manpower, more facilities, or more overtime for existing employees. This was the most expensive method of all. From this replanning effort, the program was reduced to a nine-month lead time with extremely high risk.

A report was then prepared by the network analyst which indicated the revised project definition and the new assumptions and uncertainties in the new high-risk plan. This report, along with copies of the network, total project schedule, and individual department schedules, was distributed to top management and the members of the project team.

Because of the risks in the program, updated progress information was obtained every two weeks from each member of the project team. The revised data on project status (completions, slippages, and changes) were coded, punched, and run on the computer to obtain new schedules for the project which indicated the effects of the status information. When negative slack appeared on the critical path, replanning meetings were held with executives from each department responsible for critical activities. Replanning continued until there was zero or positive slack on the critical path. At the completion of each update or replan, the network analyst would prepare a status report indicating program status, the condition of the critical path, events behind schedule, significant activities and events in the program, and recommendations. The report was distributed to top management, major executives in the company, and team project members. The close control maintained on this project through constant updating and replanning enabled the company to launch the new product in a new package on schedule to the day, as planned nine months before. The success of launching this product into test markets on time led top management to request a detailed plan for a national test and launch of the same product assuming successful test market results. The planning and control cycles were repeated as outlined earlier.

This, then, was the process of arriving at an initial operating plan, which represented the best knowledge available at the beginning of the program—and then of achieving the objectives of the plan. As the program proceeded, more was learned, and there was therefore continuous replanning in the light of this increased knowledge. The program plan was never frozen except for its final objectives.

At this consumer products company, when a program is under way and there is slippage of predicted performance, the network analyst goes first to the individual who is technically responsible and asks him to detail the source of the difficulty and make recommendations. His recommendations are incorporated in the network and immediately analyzed in order to evaluate their effect. In other words, the man responsible is given an opportunity to do his proper job, after which the network analyst reviews the proposed changes and problems with higher management. Thus the project manager is presented with completed staff work—the picture of a problem and the predicted results of these actions as they affect the overall program.

On the other hand, analysis of the problem may show that the man responsible has extended his authority to its limits and is still unable to solve the problem; he may need additional resources or action in another functional area, or his technical judgment may indicate that a more economical solution is available in an area outside his cognizance. In cases of this type, action by his manager is called for; this will be clearly demonstrable with the aid of the network.

5

The Planning Cycle

UPON APPROVAL of a corporate development program, a qualified executive in the firm is selected as the program manager. It is his responsibility to plan, organize, motivate, integrate, direct, and control efforts to obtain a specific goal. He has available to him specialized functions from other corporate organization units outside his own department.

DEVELOPMENT OF A PROGRAM ORGANIZATION

One of his first tasks is to develop a project team: This involves selecting key individuals from other functional departments who perform their specialized skill—purchasing, engineering, research, manufacturing, and so on—and represent and coordinate their departments' efforts in the project. In addition, the program manager consults with a network analyst on systems implementation.

SYSTEMS TRAINING

For those individuals who are either new to the firm or unfamiliar with the planning and control system, a network analyst can provide training material and individual instruction in the details of the system.

Approaches to training executives in PERT planning vary with each company. Some firms provide no training at all; but such firms generally have quite simplified systems. As more sophistication enters into system design, more training is necessary. Training techniques can range from individual instruction and programmed instruction packages to full-scale one-week programs given by company planning departments.

PROJECT DEFINITION

The program manager should prepare a formal project definition for the overall program. During this phase of the planning cycle, specifications and estimates are refined, familiarity with problem details is gained by the project team, and project team contributions are incorporated into the design of the program. Specifically, the project definition

1. Describes principal objectives of the program in terms of overall development goals.
2. Describes program scope in terms of extent of activity and range of operation.
3. Describes policy, budget, circumstances, strategy, or other conditions which restrict feasible action.
4. Indicates in sequence points at which decisions will be made to go ahead or to stop work.
5. Describes alternatives available.
6. Describes open issues which must be settled before the program can proceed.

Exhibit 24 shows an example of a project definition format used in a consumer-goods-oriented firm. The project definition concept is one of the characteristics of program management. In other words, concern with an identifiable end item, product, or project is definable in terms of a specific goal. In addition, it is one of the responsibilities of program management to define product standards of performance, quality, reliability, and maintainability.

During the project definition stage of a new product project, the lack of information about the product, its market, its acceptability, its development, and other characteristics make it necessary to choose a direction and outline the opportunities available. One approach to structuring and evaluating the risks among alternative courses of action has come to be called decision tree methodology. A decision tree is a simple mathematical tool which enables a planner to consider various courses of action, assign financial results to them, modify these results by their probability, and then make comparisons. The clearest way to explain the concept is with an example.

Let us suppose we have a new cosmetic product, which, if it is successful, will represent a net gain to the company of $5 million. If it is unsuccessful, however, a $.5 million investment will be lost. In addition, if we decide not to try the new cosmetic but to continue with our old product line, the company is certain to gain $.5 million. For the present, let us ignore the matter of when these sums will be gained or lost and assume that we stand to gain $5 million, lose $.5 million, or gain $.5 million instantaneously, as soon as we make the decision. Among other things, we need to know what kind of product we have, whether it is any good, and how people will like it. Basically, we want to know what chance the product has. Let us assume that it has one chance in three of being successful and two chances in three of failing.

From Exhibit 25 we can see that, at best, for a $.5 million investment, we get a $5 million return. At worst, a $.5 million investment could lose another $1 million as well. Depending upon the size of the company, the loss could be significant and disastrous or it could be taken with little effect.

If the decision had to be made and if it could be made repeatedly, two tries out of three should make $1 million and one try out of three should lose $5 million. In the long run, each try would be worth one-third of $5 million, or $1.667 million, from which we need to deduct $.667 million. Therefore, the value of each trial would be $1 million, at a cost of $.5 million for each trial. Finally, it seems that we can "expect" a profit of $1 million if we try and $.5 million if we do not. Obviously, it is worth a try.

EXHIBIT 24.   NEW PRODUCT DEVELOPMENT—
PROJECT DEFINITION

I. OBJECTIVES AND SCOPE

   A. Describe principal objectives of the project in terms of overall development goals such as desired properties of product and package, desired market share, and significant target dates.

   B. Describe scope in terms of extent of activity and range of operation in the following areas:

      1. Marketing

         a. Market size, trends, and so on.
         b. Competitive situation.
         c. Unique characteristics of product.

      2. Product

         a. Significant technical problems of product development.
         b. Development requirement categories.
            • Raw materials.
            • Equipment.
            • Process.
            • Product.
         c. Equipment considerations.
            • Suitability of present equipment.
            • Equipment modifications required.
            • New or special equipment required.
         d. Seasonality of production.

      3. Process

         a. Significant technical problems of process development.
         b. Development requirement categories.
            • Raw materials.
            • Equipment.

      4. Facilities

         a. Special facilities required.

5. Packaging

    a. Type of packaging required.

    b. Packaging development required.
- Protection.
- Use considerations.
- Features required.

    c. Packaging characteristics.
- Structural considerations.
- Performance characteristics.
- Decoration.

    d. Design considerations.
- Identity.
- Information and attention.
- Consumer acceptance.

II. RESTRICTIONS, GROUND RULES, AND DECISION POINTS

A. Describe conditions due to

- Policy.
- Budget.
- Circumstances.
- Strategy.
- Resource availability.
- Physical or technical feasibility.

Which of these restrict feasible action? Express quantitatively where possible.

B. Define in sequence the points at which decisions must be made in order to go ahead.

- Indicate who will make each decision, what inputs will be required, and what criteria will be used.

C. Indicate in sequence the major points at which selections will be made from among alternatives.

- Indicate who will make each decision and what inputs and criteria will be used.

III. QUESTIONS TO BE RESOLVED

Describe open issues which must be settled before the program can proceed. Indicate possible approaches to resolution.

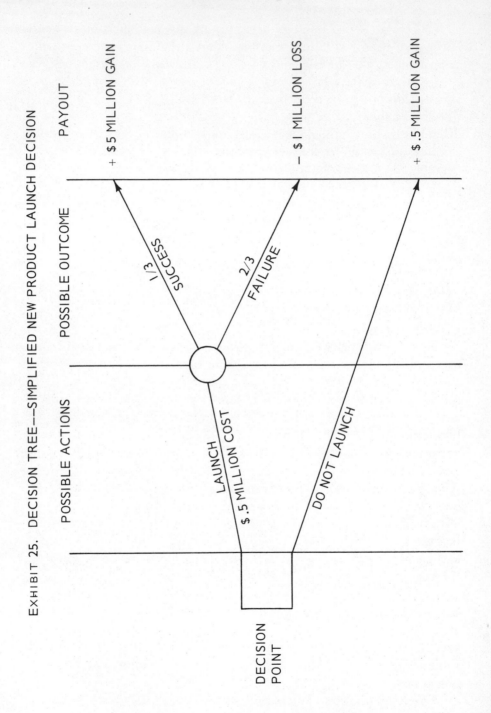

EXHIBIT 25.   DECISION TREE—SIMPLIFIED NEW PRODUCT LAUNCH DECISION

POSSIBLE ACTIONS

POSSIBLE OUTCOME

PAYOUT

DECISION
POINT

LAUNCH
$.5 MILLION COST

DO NOT LAUNCH

1/3
SUCCESS

2/3
FAILURE

+ $ 5 MILLION GAIN

− $ I MILLION LOSS

+ $ .5 MILLION GAIN

Of course, *actual* business decisions are always much more complicated than this. We do not always know how much we can make or how much we can lose, and we do not know the probabilities. We do not always have all the options; and, of course, in reality, decisions always turn out to be sequences of decisions.

The really difficult and vital elements in the construction of a decision tree are the making of assumptions and the setting of probabilities. When the word "probability" is used in connection with decision trees, it simply describes how likely we feel it is that something will happen. The chance given to any uncertain event depends on the experience of the estimator. Although the experiences of different people tend to be different, when they get together to discuss, not probabilities, but the reasons underlying them, they soon come much closer together.

WORK BREAKDOWN STRUCTURE

When project definition is complete, team members prepare task lists which indicate the work to be performed in their functional area and the inputs required from other organizational units. To aid in this effort, work breakdown structures are used to show the major tasks of the program organized in a pyramid-like fashion from the highest to the lowest level. They define the major areas of work effort and their relationships beginning with end objectives and working down to the lowest level, sometimes called the *end-item subdivision*. The substance of the work involved in each end-item subdivision must be defined in terms of performance specifications.

The development of the work breakdown structure begins at the highest level of the program with the identification of the project end items (hardware, services, equipment, facilities, or resources). The major end items are then divided into their component parts (systems, subsystems, and components), and the component parts are further divided and subdivided into more detailed units (see Exhibit 26). The subdivision of the work breakdown structure continues to successively lower levels until it reaches the level where the end-item subdivisions finally become manageable units for planning and control purposes.

The configuration and content of the work breakdown structure

EXHIBIT 26.   PRODUCT-ORIENTED WORK BREAKDOWN STRUCTURE

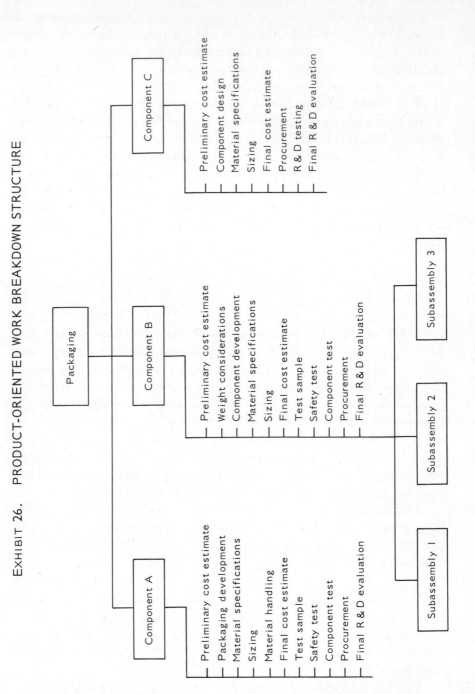

will vary from project to project and will depend on several considerations—the size and complexity of the project, the structure of the organizations concerned, and the manager's judgment concerning delegation of responsibility for the work.

Traditionally, work breakdown structures are developed on a product-oriented or functionally oriented base. A product-oriented work breakdown structure is developed on the basis of components of a product at the first level, subassemblies at the next level, parts at the next level, and so on. For example, for an automobile the levels would be chassis, then engine, then tires. The engine at the second level would include block, carburetor, and electrical system. A functionally oriented work breakdown structure is developed on the basis of functional organization structures. For example, for an automobile the first level would be design, engineering, research, manufacturing, and so on. Engineering at the second level would include mechanical engineering, automotive engineering, and electrical engineering.

For the purposes of new product programs, another approach has been developed and utilized. This approach develops the work breakdown structure on the basis of applicable company resources. At the first level of indenture are the five basic resource considerations normally found in a new product program in the consumer products industries—marketing, packaging, product, process, and facilities. All of these resources may not be necessary in every program, but one or more will be found in most programs. The marketing resource can be subdivided into the various marketing considerations in a new product program including the marketing plan, advertising, market research, sales, sales promotion, and economics. The product and packaging resources include concept, design, materials, testing, development, and economics. The process resource involves the conversion of a prototype or formula into a mass production manufacturing process and includes the engineering, design, procurement, and installation of processing facilities. Finally, the facilities resource is concerned with engineering, design, construction, installation, and start-up of facilities for the production of a consumer product. It also relates to hiring and training of production employees, start-up and debugging of equipment, and initial production of product.

Once the first, second, third, and possibly fourth level of indenture is completed, it is possible (at the lowest level) to list the tasks to be performed in order to obtain the end items. A completed work breakdown structure facilitates the development of a detailed PERT network for a new product project.

CONSTRUCTING NETWORKS

The next step is the construction of a program network. The project team meets with the program manager and the network analyst. Using the project definition formats and the completed work breakdown structure as a guide, a network is developed to show how the project objectives will be attained. During this process, inter-dependencies among the tasks or activities are identified and reflected in the network plans. As a result, the network also serves as a basis for assessing the effects of changes in any portion of the project plan as a whole. Exhibit 16 is an example of a completed network.

In new product projects where many company departments are involved, experience has shown that it is wise to set up two separate network meetings. In the first meeting, those associated with the marketing aspects of the program should formulate major program milestones and decision points which will affect all other organizations associated with the program. At the second meeting, operations organizations (engineering, manufacturing, R&D, and others) and their activities should be tied in to those major milestones and decision points developed at the first network meeting, and all interdependencies should be shown.

ESTIMATING ACTIVITY TIMES

At the present time, there are two generally accepted approaches for establishing time estimates for each activity on the network. One approach calls for a single time estimate; the other, to cope with uncertainty, requires three estimates which are then statistically converted to a single time. The choice of the one-time or three-time estimate approach should be left to the discretion of the program manager.

Generally, one-time estimates are used on activities for which, because of their repetitive nature, experience has shown that they can be accomplished within a known period of time—for example, delivery lead times on standard raw materials. Three-time estimates are generally used on activities of a highly uncertain nature where there is little past experience on which to base the estimate. Here the technical judgment and knowledge of the estimator are the basis for the three estimates (which should not be considered a commitment). The statistically calculated single time represents a 50 percent chance of being complete within that time; of course, there is also a 50 percent chance of *not* being complete. With activities of great uncertainty, such as researching a new formula or successfully completing a lab test, this kind of information may be the best that can be obtained at the beginning of a new product program.

NETWORK CHECKLISTS AND REVIEW

The accumulated experience of many networks should result in the development of network checklists for each major functional organization. These checklists contain generalized activities performed by each major organization involved in a new product program. For example, under purchasing would be the procurement cycle; under R&D, the development cycle; under market research, the research testing cycle; and so on. The prime characteristic of checklists is that they are expressed in terms sufficiently generalized to permit their application to a series of specific projects. In this sense, "generalized" does not mean vague or lacking detail; it means the checklist includes those details that pertain to many projects and omits those details that pertain only to a single project. This is done so that each checklist can serve its intended purpose:

- To shorten the process of developing a detailed plan for handling a specific project. Every project shouldn't have to start from scratch.
- To insure that the tailored project plan covers all necessary operations on a timely basis.
- To provide a clear mapping of responsibilities and operations which helps participants to know where and how their activities fit the total project.
- To provide a visible framework within which to develop and evaluate ideas for improved performance of the new product function.

The form of the output could be an outline, a flow chart, or a network. Or it could take some other form that is pertinent to each operation involved. In any case, it should be complete and reasonably explicit. It should identify all activities and accomplishments necessary to carry out an assignment, but it should be sufficiently generalized and expanded to cover the range of activities which might be encountered in the composite of several individual assignments. If this is done properly it will serve as a guide to the preparation of a tailored plan for any specific assignment. Once checklists are completed, the operation of developing a specific plan could consist of eliminating from the generalized checklists those activities which are not applicable, adding activities to cover any unusual requirements of the assignment, and specifying the generalized items to fit the particular assignment.

In general, the bulk of the activities on any departmental checklist will have to do with technical or specialized substantive activities which are a part of the expertise or know-how within the responsible unit. However, since the value of the performance on any assignment is largely a factor of timeliness and suitability in relation to the needs in other areas, it is necessary to give specific attention to interactions with others.

For the most part, the interactions of one organizational unit with another will fall into one of these categories:

- Signals or authorizations to start action; for example, go/no-go decisions.
- Communication of findings or developments which may affect the timing or content of what others are doing or planning to do. (Timeliness of these interactions is important.)
- Obtaining approvals.
- Actions to be taken at the completion of the assignment.
- Search for feedback to insure satisfactory technical performance, understanding, or assurance of transfer of the completed assignment.

The specific interactions in each area should be identified.

Within the framework of the planning and control system, as each new product network is completed, each departmental checklist should be reviewed by the network analyst and the program manager in order to be certain that all necessary activities and interactions are included in the program network.

PRELIMINARY SCHEDULE REVIEW

Once a network is completed and checked, a schedule for the program can be developed either manually or on the computer. The activities on each network are then transcribed to input forms by the scheduling staff group for keypunching input cards for a computer run. The schedule can be developed manually depending on the size and complexity of the network, but schedules developed from data processing equipment allow greater flexibility. The cards are then processed through a PERT computer program.

A typical PERT computer program performs the following functions:

- Lists the sequence of events.
- Determines the characteristics of the probability curve for performance time of activities (where three-time estimates are used).
- Synthesizes network and time data to indicate the relation to program deadlines.
- Indicates critical areas of slack.
- Compares current forecasts against scheduled completion dates and computes the probability of meeting the scheduled dates.
- Provides top management, at any time, with a summary of progress and the outlook for future progress.
- Rapidly computes the effects of alternate courses of action.

The computer output formats provide such different basic types of output reports as: (1) numerical event sort by successor event, (2) slack sort by expected date of activity, and (3) organizational sort by expected date.

The numerical event sort (Exhibit 27) acts as an activity listing or catalog and provides an easy way of finding scheduled dates for specific events or activities on the network. Since every event in a network is numbered for reference, this sort enables quick identification of any event's schedule information. Its most important use is

Exhibit 27. OUTPUT REPORT: NUMERICAL EVENT SORT BY SUCCESSOR EVENT

CRIT. PATH	PRED. EVENT	CRIT. NEIGHBOR	SUCC. EVENT	EXPECTED DATE	LATEST DATE	COMPLTED DATE	A 3	EXP TIME
*	00 001	*	00 002	02/15/68	02/15/68			02.0
	00 002	*	00 003	02/29/68	12/12/68			02.0
*	00 002	*	00 004	03/28/68	03/28/68			06.0
	00 002	*	00 005	03/14/68	07/18/68			04.0
	00 002	*	00 006	03/14/68	07/18/68			04.0
	00 006		00 007	03/14/68	07/18/68			00.0
	00 005		00 007	03/14/68	07/18/68			00.0
	00 002		00 007	04/18/68	07/18/68			09.0
*	00 004	*	00 007	07/18/68	07/18/68			16.0
*	00 007	*	00 008	09/26/68	09/26/68			10.0
	00 007		00 009	07/25/68	10/24/68			01.0
	00 008	*	00 009	09/26/68	10/24/68			00.0
	00 007	*	00 010	08/01/68	08/29/68			02.0
	00 010	*	00 011	08/15/68	09/12/68			02.0
	00 011	*	00 012	09/26/68	10/24/68			06.0
	00 008	*	00 013	10/10/68	10/24/68			02.0
	00 008	*	00 014	10/10/68	10/24/68			02.0
	00 012		00 015	09/26/68	10/24/68			00.0
	00 013		00 015	10/10/68	10/24/68			00.0
	00 014		00 015	10/10/68	10/24/68			00.0
*	00 008	*	00 015	10/24/68	10/24/68			04.0
*	00 015	*	00 016	11/21/68	11/21/68			04.0
*	00 016	*	00 017	12/19/68	12/19/68			04.0
	00 003		00 018	03/07/68	12/19/68			01.0
	00 012		00 018	10/10/68	12/19/68			02.0
	00 009		00 018	11/21/68	12/19/68			08.0
	00 016		00 018	12/05/68	12/19/68			02.0
*	00 017	*	00 018	12/19/68	12/19/68			00.0
*	00 018	*	00 019	12/26/68	12/26/68			01.0
*	00 019	*	00 020	02/27/69	02/27/69			09.0
	00 019	*	00 021	01/02/69	04/24/69			01.0
	00 019	*	00 022	01/02/69	04/24/69			01.0
	00 019	*	00 023	02/06/69	06/05/69			06.0
	00 019	*	00 024	01/23/69	03/12/70			04.0
	00 019	*	00 025	01/09/69	02/26/70			02.0
	00 021		00 026	01/02/69	04/24/69			00.0
	00 019		00 026	04/17/69	04/24/69			16.0
*	00 020	*	00 026	04/24/69	04/24/69			08.0
	00 022	*	00 027	01/30/69	05/22/69			04.0
	00 022	*	00 028	01/30/69	05/22/69			04.0
	00 027	*	00 028	01/30/69	05/22/69			00.0
*	00 026	*	00 029	06/19/69	06/19/69			08.0
	00 028		00 030	02/27/69	06/19/69			04.0
*	00 029	*	00 030	06/19/69	06/19/69			00.0
	00 023		00 031	03/06/69	07/03/69			04.0
*	00 030	*	00 031	07/03/69	07/03/69			02.0
*	00 031	*	00 032	10/23/69	10/23/69			16.0
*	00 032	*	00 033	11/06/69	11/06/69			02.0

PERT NETWORK NO. 45   NEW PRODUCT INTRODUCTION   PAGE   1
STARTING DATE 02/01/68

PROJECT ENGINEER D UMAN   DEPT. MOAD   SUBMITTED 02/15/68
BY SUCCESSOR EVENT AND COMPLETED OR EXPECTED DATE

SLACK TIME	STD DEV	PROB	ACTIVITY DESCRIPTION	
00.0	00.0		INITIAL SCREENING	A
41.0	00.0		CHECK PRODT CONFORMANCE TO GOVT REGUL	D
00.0	00.0		INDUSTRIAL DESIGN	M
18.0	00.0		ADVERTISING SUGGESTIONS	N
18.0	00.0		SALES SUGGESTIONS	Q
18.0	00.0			
18.0	00.0			
13.0	00.0		MOTIVATION RESEARCH	L
00.0	00.0		RESEARCH & DEVELOPMENT ON MODEL	B
00.0	00.0		BUILD CRUDE MODEL	M
13.0	00.0		EXECUTIVE REACTIONS	A
04.0	00.0			
04.0	00.0		ESTIMATE MARKET CHARACTERISTICS	A
04.0	00.0		ESTIMATE COMPETITIVE BEHAVIOR	A
04.0	00.0		ESTIMATE MARKET POTENTIAL	A
02.0	00.0		ESTIMATE DISTRIBUTION COSTS	A
02.0	00.0		ESTIMATE ADVERTISING COSTS	N
04.0	00.0			
02.0	00.0			
02.0	00.0			
00.0	00.0		ESTIMATE MANUFACTURING COSTS	D
00.0	00.0		PRICE VS DEMAND CURVE	A
00.0	00.0		PRELIMINARY FINANCIAL ANALYSIS	A
41.0	00.0		CHECK PRODT NON-VIOLATION OF PATENTS	A
10.0	00.0		REVIEW MANUFACTURING FACILITIES	D
04.0	00.0		CONSUMER REACTIONS	L
02.0	00.0		PRELIMINARY PRICE RANGE	A
00.0	00.0			
00.0	00.0		FULL-SCALE TEST DECISION	A
00.0	00.0		COMPLETE PRODUCT DESIGN	M
16.0	00.0		BUY RAW MATERIALS	G
16.0	00.0		SAMPLING TECHNIQUES	L
17.0	00.0		PRELIMINARY ADVERTISING COPY	N
59.0	00.0		PRELIMINARY SALES PLANS	Q
59.0	00.0		DETERMINE FINANCIAL NEEDS	A
16.0	00.0			
01.0	00.0		EQUIPMENT FOR MANUFACTURING NEEDS	D
00.0	00.0		ENGINEERING LAB TEST	M
16.0	00.0		SET-UP SAMPLES FOR MARKET TESTING	M
16.0	00.0		MARKET TEST FORMS PREPARED	L
16.0	00.0			
00.0	00.0		MANUFACTURE MODELS	D
16.0	00.0		GET INTERVIEWERS	L
00.0	00.0			
17.0	00.0		PRELIMINARY MEDIA EVALUATION	A
00.0	00.0		TRAIN INTERVIEWERS	L
00.0	00.0		MARKET TEST	A
00.0	00.0		CODE & TABULATE TEST	L

by members of functional departments who want to determine schedules for interacting departments.

The slack sort by expected date of activity (Exhibit 28) lists all the paths on a network starting with the critical path. It lists events in slack sequence from the least positive—or most negative—to the most positive. This listing is the major analytical tool of the system because it focuses attention on the critical aspects of a program.

The organizational sort by expected date (Exhibit 29) lists all the activities by functional department and chronological expected dates. For example, the purchasing department will receive a schedule of all the program events it is responsible for on each program, with the events listed in chronological order of expected completion dates.

Each page of the computer output has columns for each activity—critical path, expected completion date, latest date the activity can occur before it becomes critical, actual completion date of completed activities, activity time, slack (difference between scheduled and latest completion dates), and activity title.

By imposing a directed completion date on the end event in the computer run, one can measure the effect of the network plan on this date. If the critical path has a completion date later than the directed completion date, the program has *negative slack;* that is, a behind-schedule condition.

The amount of slack in the network should be reviewed and analyzed. If negative slack exists, a recommendation is made for a replan. In addition, each team member should review his schedule and report feasibility or recommend changes.

REVIEWING AND REVISING THE PLAN

If program replanning is required, an analysis of slack and the critical path will show where time must be reduced. Those members of the project team whose activities are on the critical path should attend a replanning meeting at which the network is revised until the completion date is simultaneous with the directed completion date. This generally implies that team members must compromise on network configuration, and additional risk must be accepted in order to complete the project on schedule.

Replanning generally requires reducing time along various paths in a network. It is safe to assume that activity time estimates are reliable if they are given by those performing the work. Therefore, in replanning, activity times are not reduced. Once submitted, time estimates should not change unless there are resource changes or other knowledge which would change estimates. These changes include revision of plans, introduction of new resources, change in personnel, technical difficulties or breakthroughs, and authorization of overtime. Time can be reduced in a network by

1. Changing the sequence of events from series to parallel.
2. Changing the scope of activities or of the project.
3. Applying such resources to the project as money, manpower, materials, and space.
4. Eliminating certain events.

At this point, particularly in large programs, the network analyst may wish to run through a number of *simulation exercises* to determine the exact effect on critical path outcome of changing activity sequences or transferring resources.

A simulation exercise determines the outlook or impact of major changes in the planned approach. An example of a simulation exercise occurred in the consumer products company cited earlier after the first network was prepared. The initial computer run showed that the product being improved would take two years to reach national distribution if a two-city test market was attempted. At a suggestion from the network analyst, a simulation run was made reflecting the effect on the schedule of eliminating the test market. When it was shown that by accepting additional risk the program could be reduced to nine months, management made the decision to eliminate the requirement for the test market because of competitive pressure. This kind of information presented to management early in a program enables greater flexibility and allows decision making based on completed staff work.

The role of the network analyst at the replanning meeting is to make sure that the basic ground rules for replanning are followed. The final decisions made during replanning are properly the responsibility of management, not of the network analyst.

EXHIBIT 28. OUTPUT REPORT: SLACK SORT BY EXPECTED DATE OF ACTIVITY

CRIT. PATH	PRED. EVENT	CRIT. NEIGHBOR	SUCC. EVENT	EXPECTED DATE	LATEST DATE	COMPLTED DATE	A S	EXP TIME
*	00 001	*	00 002	02/15/68	02/15/68			02.0
*	00 002	*	00 004	03/28/68	03/28/68			06.0
*	00 004	*	00 007	07/18/68	07/18/68			16.0
*	00 007	*	00 008	09/26/68	09/26/68			10.0
*	00 008	*	00 015	10/24/68	10/24/68			04.0
*	00 015	*	00 016	11/21/68	11/21/68			04.0
*	00 016	*	00 017	12/19/68	12/19/68			04.0
*	00 017	*	00 018	12/19/68	12/19/68			00.0
*	00 018	*	00 019	12/26/68	12/26/68			01.0
*	00 019	*	00 020	02/27/69	02/27/69			09.0
*	00 020	*	00 026	04/24/69	04/24/69			08.0
*	00 026	*	00 029	06/19/69	06/19/69			08.0
*	00 029	*	00 030	06/19/69	06/19/69			00.0
*	00 030	*	00 031	07/03/69	07/03/69			02.0
*	00 031	*	00 032	10/23/69	10/23/69			16.0
*	00 032	*	00 033	11/06/69	11/06/69			02.0
*	00 033	*	00 034	11/20/69	11/20/69			02.0
*	00 034	*	00 035	11/20/69	11/20/69			00.0
*	00 035	*	00 038	03/12/70	03/12/70			16.0
*	00 038	*	00 039	03/16/70	03/16/70			00.5
*	00 039	*	00 049	05/25/70	05/25/70			10.0
*	00 049	*	00 055	06/22/70	06/22/70			04.0
*	00 055	*	00 056	07/20/70	07/20/70			04.0
*	00 056	*	00 059	08/17/70	08/17/70			04.0
*	00 059	*	00 060	09/14/70	09/14/70			04.0
*	00 060	*	00 062	09/21/70	09/21/70			01.0
*	00 062	*	00 063	09/21/70	09/21/70			00.0
	00 019		00 026	04/17/69	04/24/69			16.0
	00 049	*	00 054	05/28/70	06/08/70			00.5
	00 054		00 056	07/09/70	07/20/70			06.0
	00 008	*	00 013	10/10/68	10/24/68			02.0
	00 008	*	00 014	10/10/68	10/24/68			02.0
	00 013		00 015	10/10/68	10/24/68			00.0
	00 014		00 015	10/10/68	10/24/68			00.0
	00 016		00 018	12/05/68	12/19/68			02.0
	00 034	*	00 036	01/29/70	02/12/70			10.0
	00 036	*	00 037	02/12/70	02/26/70			02.0
	00 036		00 038	02/26/70	03/12/70			04.0
	00 037		00 038	02/26/70	03/12/70			02.0
	00 049	*	00 053	05/28/70	06/22/70			00.5
	00 053		00 056	06/25/70	07/20/70			04.0
	00 007	*	00 010	08/01/68	08/29/68			02.0
	00 010	*	00 011	08/15/68	09/12/68			02.0
	00 008	*	00 009	09/26/68	10/24/68			00.0
	00 011	*	00 012	09/26/68	10/24/68			06.0
	00 012		00 015	09/26/68	10/24/68			00.0
	00 009		00 018	11/21/68	12/19/68			08.0
	00 039	*	00 042	03/30/70	04/27/70			02.0

PERT NETWORK NO. 45   NEW PRODUCT INTRODUCTION   PAGE   1
STARTING DATE 02/01/68
PROJECT ENGINEER D UMAN   DEPT. MOAD   SUBMITTED 02/15/68
BY SLACK TIME AND COMPLETED OR EXPECTED DATE

SLACK TIME	STD DEV	PROB	ACTIVITY DESCRIPTION	
00.0	00.0		INITIAL SCREENING	A
00.0	00.0		INDUSTRIAL DESIGN	M
00.0	00.0		RESEARCH & DEVELOPMENT ON MODEL	B
00.0	00.0		BUILD CRUDE MODEL	M
00.0	00.0		ESTIMATE MANUFACTURING COSTS	D
00.0	00.0		PRICE VS DEMAND CURVE	A
00.0	00.0		PRELIMINARY FINANCIAL ANALYSIS	A
00.0	00.0			
00.0	00.0		FULL-SCALE TEST DECISION	A
00.0	00.0		COMPLETE PRODUCT DESIGN	M
00.0	00.0		ENGINEERING LAB TEST	M
00.0	00.0		MANUFACTURE MODELS	D
00.0	00.0			
00.0	00.0		TRAIN INTERVIEWERS	L
00.0	00.0		MARKET TEST	A
00.0	00.0		CODE & TABULATE TEST	L
00.0	00.0		EVALUATE TEST RESULTS	A
00.0	00.0			
00.0	00.0		INVESTIGATE NAMES & LABELS	A
00.0	00.0		MANAGEMENT GO-AHEAD DECISION	A
00.0	00.0		DESIGN LABEL & TRADEMARK	F
00.0	00.0		HIRE WORKERS	E
00.0	00.0		TRAIN WORKERS	E
00.0	00.0		FULL-SCALE MANUFACTURING	E
00.0	00.0		SELL TO OUTLETS	Q
00.0	00.0		SHIP TO DISTRIBUTORS	E
00.0	00.0		INTRODUCE NEW PRODUCT	A
01.0	00.0		EQUIPMENT FOR MANUFACTURING NEEDS	D
01.5	00.0		ORDER RAW MATERIALS	G
01.5	00.0		RECEIVE RAW MATERIALS	E
02.0	00.0		ESTIMATE DISTRIBUTION COSTS	A
02.0	00.0		ESTIMATE ADVERTISING COSTS	N
02.0	00.0			
02.0	00.0		PRELIMINARY PRICE RANGE	A
02.0	00.0		IMPROVE PRODUCT	B
02.0	00.0		ESTABLISH QUALITY CONTROL	D
02.0	00.0		INVESTIGATE PATENT APPLICATION	A
02.0	00.0		PLAN MANUFACTURING	D
03.5	00.0		EQUIPMENT PURCHASE	G
03.5	00.0		SET UP EQUIPMENT	E
04.0	00.0		ESTIMATE MARKET CHARACTERISTICS	A
04.0	00.0		ESTIMATE COMPETITIVE BEHAVIOR	A
04.0	00.0			
04.0	00.0		ESTIMATE MARKET POTENTIAL	A
04.0	00.0			
04.0	00.0		CONSUMER REACTIONS	L
04.0	00.0		DETERMINE SEASONAL DEMAND	A

Exhibit 29.   OUTPUT REPORT: ORGANIZATIONAL SORT BY EXPECTED DATE

PERT NETWORK NO.   45   NEW PRODUCT INTRODUCTION   PAGE 1

STARTING DATE 02/01/68 | SUBMITTED 02/15/68

CRIT. PATH	PRED. EVENT	CRIT. NEIGHBOR	SUCC. EVENT	EXPECTED DATE	LATEST DATE	COMPLTED DATE	A S	EXP TIME
*	00 001	*	00 002	02/15/68	02/15/68			02.0
	00 003		00 018	03/07/68	12/19/68			01.0
	00 007		00 009	07/25/68	10/24/68			01.0
	00 007	*	00 010	08/01/68	08/29/68			02.0
	00 010	*	00 011	08/15/68	09/12/68			02.0
	00 011	*	00 012	09/26/68	10/24/68			06.0
	00 008	*	00 013	10/10/68	10/24/68			02.0
*	00 015	*	00 016	11/21/68	11/21/68			04.0
	00 016		00 018	12/05/68	12/19/68			02.0
*	00 016	*	00 017	12/19/68	12/19/68			04.0
*	00 018	*	00 019	12/26/68	12/26/68			01.0
	00 019	*	00 025	01/09/69	02/26/70			02.0
	00 025		00 038	01/23/69	03/12/70			02.0
	00 023		00 031	03/06/69	07/03/69			04.0
	00 029		00 040	07/03/69	07/20/70			02.0
*	00 031	*	00 032	10/23/69	10/23/69			16.0
*	00 033	*	00 034	11/20/69	11/20/69			02.0
	00 036		00 038	02/26/70	03/12/70			04.0
*	00 035	*	00 038	03/12/70	03/12/70			16.0
*	00 038	*	00 039	03/16/70	03/16/70			00.5
	00 039	*	00 048	03/23/70	05/25/70			01.0
	00 039	*	00 042	03/30/70	04/27/70			02.0
	00 039		00 050	03/30/70	06/22/70			02.0
	00 040	*	00 058	03/30/70	08/03/70			02.0
	00 039	*	00 044	03/30/70	08/10/70			02.0
	00 039		00 045	03/30/70	08/10/70			02.0
	00 039	*	00 041	03/30/70	09/21/70			02.0
	00 042	*	00 046	04/13/70	05/11/70			02.0
	00 042		00 045	04/13/70	08/10/70			02.0
	00 058		00 059	04/13/70	08/17/70			02.0
	00 058	*	00 061	04/13/70	09/07/70			02.0
	00 046		00 049	04/27/70	05/25/70			02.0
	00 043	*	00 045	05/18/70	08/10/70			01.0
	00 045		00 052	05/25/70	08/24/70			01.0
	00 045	*	00 051	06/01/70	08/24/70			02.0
*	00 062	*	00 063	09/21/70	09/21/70			00.0

PROJECT ENGINEER D UMAN DEPT. MOAD

BY DEPARTMENT, COMPLETED OR EXPECTED DATE, SCHEDULED OR

LATEST DATE, AND SUCCESSOR EVENT

PRODUCT DIVISION-PRODUCT MANAGER

SLACK TIME	STD DEV	PROB	ACTIVITY DESCRIPTION	
00.0	00.0		INITIAL SCREENING	A
41.0	00.0		CHECK PRODT NON-VIOLATION OF PATENTS	A
13.0	00.0		EXECUTIVE REACTIONS	A
04.0	00.0		ESTIMATE MARKET CHARACTERISTICS	A
04.0	00.0		ESTIMATE COMPETITIVE BEHAVIOR	A
04.0	00.0		ESTIMATE MARKET POTENTIAL	A
02.0	00.0		ESTIMATE DISTRIBUTION COSTS	A
00.0	00.0		PRICE VS DEMAND CURVE	A
02.0	00.0		PRELIMINARY PRICE RANGE	A
00.0	00.0		PRELIMINARY FINANCIAL ANALYSIS	A
00.0	00.0		FULL-SCALE TEST DECISION	A
59.0	00.0		DETERMINE FINANCIAL NEEDS	A
59.0	00.0		FINANCIAL FORECAST	A
17.0	00.0		PRELIMINARY MEDIA EVALUATION	A
54.5	00.0		INVESTIGATE DISTRIBUTION	A
00.0	00.0		MARKET TEST	A
00.0	00.0		EVALUATE TEST RESULTS	A
02.0	00.0		INVESTIGATE PATENT APPLICATION	A
00.0	00.0		INVESTIGATE NAMES & LABELS	A
00.0	00.0		MANAGEMENT GO-AHEAD DECISION	A
09.0	00.0		SELECT NAME	A
04.0	00.0		DETERMINE SEASONAL DEMAND	A
12.0	00.0		SELECT SALES MANAGER	A
18.0	00.0		SELECT DISTRIBUTION CHANNELS	A
19.0	00.0		SET ADVERTISING BUDGET	A
19.0	00.0		EVALUATE MEDIA	A
25.0	00.0		PATENT APPLICATION SUBMITTED	A
04.0	00.0		ESTABLISH PRICES	A
17.0	00.0		ESTABLISH PRICES	A
18.0	00.0		ESTABLISH DISTRIBUTION CHANNELS	A
21.0	00.0		DETERMINE SERVICE NEEDS	A
04.0	00.0		FINANCIAL FUNDS FLOW FORECAST	A
12.0	00.0		SELECT ADVERTISING COPY	A
13.0	00.0		SELECT MEDIA	A
12.0	00.0		SELECT PROMOTIONAL AIDS	A
00.0	00.0		INTRODUCE NEW PRODUCT	A

Developing the Final Plan

When the network changes are complete, they are transcribed to input for a computer run. The new output reports are reviewed again, and, if satisfactory, the final plan is fixed. If it is not satisfactory, replanning continues until all negative slack is eliminated or a satisfactory schedule is arrived at.

When the final plan is fixed, it is a good idea for the network analyst or program manager to prepare a report which summarizes all the areas in the program plan where assumptions were made, exceptions to company policy were taken, and exceptional risks were absorbed in order to complete a satisfactory plan. This report and copies of the program network should be distributed to all executives and team members involved, including top management. This kind of report allows further discussion and evaluation of the plan and clarifies the assumptions, exceptions, and risks associated with it.

6

The Control Cycle

AFTER PLANNING is completed, the program manager reviews the final plan and approves the schedule. A final draft of the network is prepared by a draftsman for eventual distribution to the team members.

Each member of the project team then receives a copy of the network, a numerical sort (activity listing), and a copy of his organizational sort by expected date. At this point, he has all the information about the product development project he needs in order to perform his portion of the program. This schedule constitutes the time plan for the project until such time as a change is required owing to slippages in the work, changes in the network, or changes in resource availability.

UPDATING THE PLAN

As a new product development project progresses, work activities are added or deleted, work is completed behind or ahead of schedule, and time estimates for unfinished work are revised. Updating procedures are therefore required that will facilitate change caused by new estimates, estimates to complete work in process, and latest revised estimates for work not yet begun. This product development planning and control system provides systematic updating by establishing specific review dates, requiring estimate preparation and revision, and requiring time re-estimates on an exception basis when current information indicates changes are needed in the initial estimates of time and other resources.

An updating procedure should be prepared that includes a complete description of how updating information is prepared and handled, who receives the information, and how it is used. Within this system, five kinds of periodic project status information are required on the activities in a project (see Exhibit 30):

1. Activities completed.
2. Activities started, but not yet completed.
3. Activities that should have been started but have not been.
4. Activities that should be deleted (because of changes in the project).
5. Activities that should be added (because of changes in the project).

This information is generally forwarded to the network analyst, who reviews the data for significant changes in the program. What is of interest here is the impact of these changes on the schedule, cost, and performance of the program over time. Once a computer run reflecting these changes is obtained, a status report is prepared for management. Should there be problems in the project schedule, additional analytical tools are available.

PREPARING THE STATUS REPORT

This change information is transcribed onto input formats for new computer runs. After analysis, a status report is prepared (Exhibit 31) which should indicate the following:

1. Amount of slippage in the program.
2. Activities and events behind schedule.

3. Critical path activities.
4. Significant activities or events.
5. Recommendations for program improvement.
6. Summary of slack over time.

This type of report provides necessary program status information to higher management. Program slippage indicates what part of the program is critical, who is responsible, how much schedule slippage exists, and which events and activities are behind schedule. A list of critical path events, their elapsed times, and responsible organizations should be included to allow management to review the sequence of critical events along the longest path. Attention must be drawn to these events because they must be completed on time or the whole program schedule will be affected.

The status report has a section indicating significant events and activities in the program. A description of which events had the most slippage and why, events that were added and deleted and why, and critical aspects of the program should be included here. The report should include recommendations to management as to what can be done about program schedule problems.

The slack summary (Exhibit 32) shows graphically the amount of positive (ahead of schedule) or negative (behind schedule) slack that exists in a program over time. In addition, the scheduled completion date is shown on a scale of weeks to scheduled completion date.

EVALUATING PROJECT STATUS

Project status is then evaluated by the program manager and the network analyst to identify the schedule problem area. On the basis of this evaluation, the program manager may take alternative action to minimize costs and avoid schedule slippages:

1. Adjust the schedule of slack path activities to minimize the need for overtime or additional hiring.
2. Revise network sequence or content by
   a. Employing a greater or lesser amount of parallelism in performing activities.
   b. Modifying the specifications or method of performing the work, thereby altering, deleting, or adding activities.

Exhibit 30.   NETWORK UPDATING PROCEDURE

A. All participants should indicate on their department schedule in the column marked "COMP." the following information:

1. If an activity is complete, enter date completed. See ①.

2. If an activity has begun but is not yet complete, enter date expected to complete. Add a brief explanation. See ②.

3. If an activity should have started but has not, enter "NOT START-ED." Add a brief explanation. See ③.

4. If an activity should be deleted, enter "DELETE" and state why. See ④.

5. If activities should be added, enter "INSERT" with an activity description and estimate of activity duration. Indicate existing event numbers which precede and follow the inserted activity. See ⑤.

EXAMPLE

Prec. Event	Succ. Event	Dates Exp.	Latest	Comp.	Exp. Time	Activity Description	
530	540	6/19/68	6/19/68	6/19	01.0	PO Cartons C	①
540	550	6/19/68	6/26/68	7/15	01.0	Plates C	②
550	560	6/26/71	7/07/68	*Not started*	04.0	Commercial Prodn C	③
~~560~~	~~570~~	~~7/03/68~~	~~7/22/68~~	*Delete*	~~03.0~~	~~Commercial Test C~~	④
560	*590*			*Insert*	*05.0*	*Prepare answer print*	⑤

REMARKS:

540-550 - Vendor delay; 560-570 Test cancelled; 550-560 - Awaiting go-ahead approval

B. Please review all activity times on your schedule and indicate any changes with a brief explanation.

EXHIBIT 31. UPDATE I STATUS REPORT

1. Program Status and Critical Path

   A. PERT analysis indicates that the overall program is predicted to be 1.4 weeks <u>behind</u> schedule.

   B. The following activities are behind schedule (latest date not met) and were reported not complete as of this update.

Respons.	Prec. Event	Succ. Event	Activity	Exp. Date	Latest Date
Mktg	01	25	Creative Development	10/23/68	10/13/68
Mktg	30	70	Network Approval Start	10/27/68	10/27/68
Mktg	70	120	Network Approval Complete	11/03/68	11/03/68
Mktg	130	200	Prepare Sales Materials	10/23/68	10/24/68
Mktg	200	250	Sales Materials Approved	10/30/68	10/31/68
Mktg	250	350	Purchase Order Sales Materials	10/30/68	10/31/68

   C. The critical path is through the following events:

Prec. Event	Succ. Event	Activity Time	Activity	Respons.
01	25	15.0	Creative Development	Mktg
30	70	1.0	Network Approval Start	Mktg
70	120	1.0	Network Approval Complete	Mktg
120	240	3.0	Commercial Production	Agency
240	340	2.0	Rough Cut Revisions	Agency
340	400	1.0	View Print and Approval	Mktg
400	470	3.0	Test Commercial	Agency
470	550	1.0	Commercial Test Results	Agency
550	700	3.0	Distribute Films	Agency
700	710	0	Start Advertising	Mktg

2. Significant Activities and Events

   A. Analysis of slack indicates that slippage in creative development has caused the major slippage in the program.

3. Recommendations

   A. Because there is a minimum amount of slippage in program, it is recommended that major replanning wait until the next update.

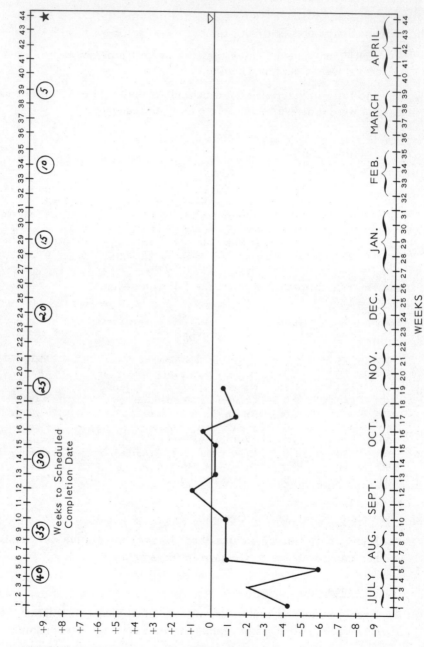

EXHIBIT 32.   PRODUCT N – SLACK SUMMARY

Since the actions that management takes to correct problems often involve revising plans, schedules, and budgets, the system cycle will be repeated periodically throughout the course of a product development program.

RECOMMENDATION OF ALTERNATE COURSES OF ACTION

At this point, additional analysis of the program may provide other alternatives for the program manager and higher management. Information is now available which can be used with the techniques of simulation, risk analysis, and capital budgeting.

Simulation is a technique frequently used by operations researchers and systems analysts in problem solving. The basis of simulation procedures is generally a model. In effect, a network is a model which will be useful in predicting, in operational terms, the outcome of planned actions in a certain sequence. With a network, we can revise, add to, or delete sequences of events in order to predict the outcome of alternative actions so that the most appropriate action can be determined.

Basically, once a reasonable alternative in a simulation exercise is arrived at from the evaluation of program status, the data are coded onto input forms, and change cards are punched. The computer run output reports show the impact of these changes on the total program schedule. Simulation exercises should continue until a feasible schedule is arrived at.

One possible conclusion is that *no* feasible alternatives exist that can maintain the project's original scheduled completion date. The great advantage of this type of project planning system is that this fact will be known early in the program or when program problems develop, not at the end of the program when lack of time or alternatives prevents remedial action. Once it is known that no feasible alternatives exist, management must decide to change the scheduled completion date, change the scope of the project, or commit additional resources (usually money)—in each case, a painful decision.

Risk analysis is the identification of alternatives and consequences to be made in a decision with the detailed analysis of individual consequence chains under conditions of certainty, risk, and uncertainty.

An evaluation scheme is necessary in order to reveal the preferred consequence chain with the most attractive consequence.

A major feature of new product programs is that deadlines are ever present and represent a troublesome aspect of the ongoing operations of any firm. It must be recognized that not many decisions can be made in an atmosphere of leisurely investigation and reflection.

These time pressures can force decisions based on less than the desired amount of information. Other pressures also act within the context of the firm to force decisions in spite of meager knowledge of the consequences. One of these pressures is cost, in particular the cost of collecting the information and carrying out the analysis of the decision. In introducing a new product, for example, it would be very useful to have the results of a thorough test market. This, however, is simply too expensive for many firms. In fact, some information just cannot be obtained at any cost—such as information about the future or certain information about a competitor's marketing strategy.

Since time and cost, together or individually, exert pressures on the decision process and consequently force decisions to be made with incomplete information and analysis, this means that fewer alternatives will be identified, and less evidence will be obtained on the outcomes, their probabilities, and their values. In the absence of this evidence, it is increasingly difficult to perform analysis. It might also be said that as pressure increases, we are more likely to find management making its decisions on the basis of judgment, unorganized experience, and the implicit processes of choice.

Risk analysis, then, is an approach to the decision-making process which can take into consideration the realistic pressures of time in evaluating alternatives, consequences, and outcomes. It utilizes concepts of modern statistics to give a decision maker a rational method of reacting to time pressure and thus enable him to maximize the expected return. Although much of risk analysis is beyond the context of this book, suffice it to say that the product development planning system facilitates its use. Within the framework of a new product network, major milestones and decision points indicate where and when decisions must be made and what inputs will be available for making each decision. A completed network lends itself to developing alternatives and structuring the analysis for decision making.

Capital budgeting decisions are obtained through analysis of total project capital costs in order to arrive at expected return on investment. Here, the advantage of the product development planning and control system is that it advises management when capital funds must be allocated over time and the extent of the risk involved in releasing capital funds.

Very often, because of the high risk and uncertainty of new product success in the marketplace, management wishes to delay the expenditure of capital funds until the latest possible date. Supposedly, this is intended to limit the extent of the investment until management either has enough information to make a decision or cannot possibly delay any longer without affecting the launch schedule. A network plan allows management under these conditions to crash a schedule—that is, to remove all positive slack along paths where there are expenditures and to determine the latest possible date when funds must be committed. When this plan is combined with risk analysis techniques (to determine the extent of the risk at the time funds must be spent and the expected payoffs of feasible alternatives), management has a powerful tool to aid the new product launch decision.

REVISING PLAN AND SCHEDULES

Based on the evaluation of project status and the additional analysis of alternatives, the project plan is revised, and an additional computer run is made for final schedules which are then distributed to the project team for action.

HIGHER MANAGEMENT REPORTS

The basic information generated by the system can be summarized in several ways for program management reporting. The format and detail in which this information is presented can vary depending upon requirements of different levels of management. Management reports make available in written and diagrammatic form the schedule and cost data needed by program management to identify present trouble spots in projects which require management analysis and action. Essentially, the reports provide management with the following information in varying degrees of detail:

EXHIBIT 33.   NETWORK MILESTONES

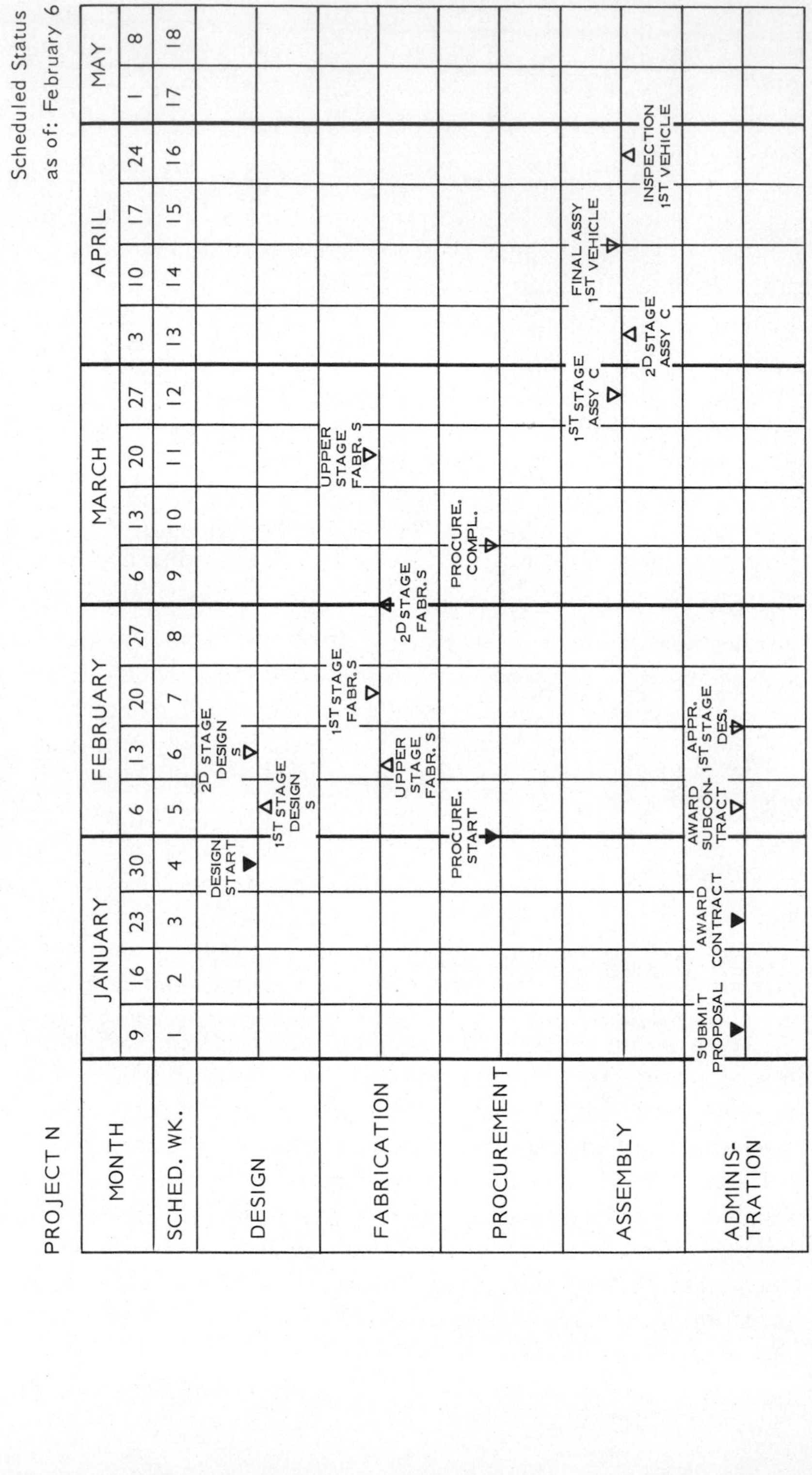

PROJECT N

Scheduled Status
as of: February 6

MONTH	JANUARY				FEBRUARY				MARCH				APRIL				MAY		
SCHED. WK.	9 1	16 2	23 3	30 4	6 5	13 6	20 7	27 8	6 9	13 10	20 11	27 12	3 13	10 14	17 15	24 16	1 17	8 18
DESIGN				DESIGN START ▶	1ST STAGE DESIGN S △	2D STAGE DESIGN S △												
FABRICATION					UPPER STAGE FABR. S △		1ST STAGE FABR. S △	2D STAGE FABR. S △			UPPER STAGE FABR. S △							
PROCUREMENT				PROCURE. START ▶					PROCURE. COMPL. ▶									
ASSEMBLY												1ST STAGE ASSY C △	2D STAGE ASSY C △	FINAL ASSY 1ST VEHICLE △		INSPECTION 1ST VEHICLE △		
ADMINIS- TRATION	SUBMIT PROPOSAL ▶		AWARD CONTRACT ▶		AWARD SUBCON- TRACT ▶	APPR. 1ST STAGE DES. ▶												

1. The current project plan and schedule.
2. Schedule performance to date, in relation to the plan.
3. Schedule projections for completion of the project objectives.

Equally important, the system reports point up potential trouble in the project and make it possible for managers to anticipate schedule slippages. In addition, they alert the program manager when his attention is needed most urgently.

Higher management reports are usually prepared on a monthly basis. However, reporting can be done more frequently, if required or desired. Additional information provided to higher management includes the slack summary shown in Exhibit 32 and a milestone chart (Exhibit 33). This chart is a ramification of the Gantt chart (Exhibit 5) with selected network events representing major milestones of accomplishment toward the completion of a program added. The milestone chart illustrated in Exhibit 33 shows the project manager each milestone scheduled over the duration of the program, each action accomplished on schedule, and each scheduled future action.

Because of the increasing complexity, cost, and risk involved in product development programs, the need for a planning and control system has been great in non-defense-system industries. As a result of new management techniques evolved within the last decade, a series of modern approaches to management planning and control have led to an integrated reporting and information system. Using network analysis as its base, the planning cycle and a control cycle of the product development planning and control system give a program manager a tool that readily satisfies his requirements for information and organization. The benefits to be obtained from this approach are substantial. The resulting improvements in planning and control of programs within original time and cost estimates and with increases in efficiency go a long way toward increasing the profits of any firm that uses it.

Appendix

PERT Mathematical Concepts

THIS APPENDIX explains, in sufficient detail, the mathematics for the three-time estimate calculations and the standard deviation and range. All basic information has been derived from the *AFSC PERT Policies and Procedures Handbook.*[1]

Three-Time Estimates

The three-time estimate is used to define a probability distribution. This is just a quantitative way of handling the uncertainty of the estimator and thus permitting statements about the likelihood that the activity will be completed in a time span which is anywhere in the range between the optimistic and pessimistic time. For instance, we can state the probability that an activity will be completed earlier or later than the computed time derived in the next paragraph.

Exhibit 34 illustrates a beta probability distribution and shows how it is defined by the three-time estimate. A beta distribution was chosen

[1] *AFSC PERT Policies and Procedures Handbook*, ASD Exhibit ASOO 61-1 (Washington, D.C.: Aeronautical Systems Division, AFSC, January 6, 1962), pp. II-14 —II-17.

EXHIBIT 34.   BETA PROBABILITY DISTRIBUTION

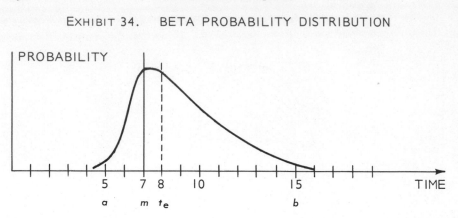

because it is easy to use in conjunction with the three estimates, some relatively easy and good approximations can be made when handling it mathematically, and it does not violate any intuitions we may have about the character of uncertain activities.

The optimistic, most likely, and pessimistic time span estimates are shown as the left extreme, the mode (highest point on the curve), and the right extreme, respectively. The height of the line from the base line (or time axis) to the curve is a relative measure of the probability that the activity will take the time in question. We see that there is little chance of the activity taking 5 or 15 weeks (the vertical line to the curve is short), and that it is most likely to take 6 or 7 weeks (the vertical lines to the curve are long).

The calculated activity time (t_e) of the distribution is found by a simple approximation formula and falls one-third of the way between the most likely time and the midpoint between the optimistic and pessimistic time (here, between 7 and 10). The t_e is a point (8 in this example) such that there is a 50 percent chance that the time span will, in fact, prove to be shorter and a 50 percent chance that the time span will, in fact, prove to be longer than the calculated time span.

By using the beta distribution, we get a mean value that is usually to the pessimistic side of the most likely time (which occurs when the most likely time is closer to the optimistic than the pessimistic time). This yields a conservative time estimate.

THE STANDARD DEVIATION

The standard deviation, sigma (σ), here approximated simply by one-sixth of the time between the optimistic and pessimistic points ($b - a$) ÷ 6 (in the example, $15 - 5 \div 6 = 1.6$), is a quantitative expres-

EXHIBIT 35. STANDARD DEVIATION AND RANGE

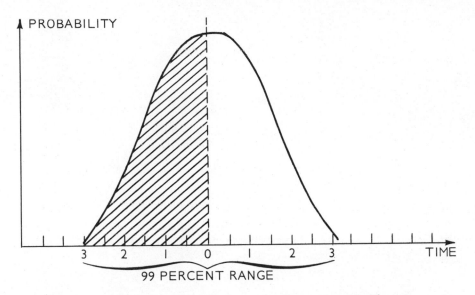

sion of the uncertainty which the manager has expressed. If we were to go three standard deviations in each direction from the mean value, we would encompass a range in which we would be 99 percent certain to include the span which will actually occur. This is shown in Exhibit 35.

Another useful property of the probability distribution curve is that the area under the curve, to the left of any vertical line, gives a measure of how likely the time span is to be *equal to or less than* the time in question. In Exhibit 35, the shaded area to the left of the mean says that there is a 50 percent chance that the time span for this activity will turn out to be *less than or equal to* eight weeks (the total area under the curve is 100 percent).

Exhibit 35 depicts a normal or bell-shaped distribution. In the PERT system, the beta distribution is used only as a method to get a mean and standard deviation from the three-time estimates. The mean and standard deviations are then used to define normal distributions which are approximations to the beta distribution and are much easier to work with, mathematically, in the network. The mathematics to substantiate this philosophy and the justification of this procedure are discussed in such sources as *Schedule, Cost and Profit with PERT*[2] and *PERT Summary Report Phase I.*[3]

[2] Robert W. Miller, *Schedule, Cost and Profit Control with PERT* (New York: McGraw-Hill Book Company, 1963), pp. 199–201.
[3] *PERT Summary Report Phase I*, Navy Special Projects Office (Washington, D.C.: U.S. Government Printing Office, 1960).

Suggested Additional Reading

Adler, Lee, "Systems Approach to Marketing," *Harvard Business Review*, (May/June 1967), p. 105.

American Management Association, *New Products/New Profits* (New York: American Management Association, Inc.), 1964.

———, *Establishing a New Product Program*, AMA Management Report No. 8, 1958.

———, *Organizing for Product Development*, AMA Management Report No. 31, 1959.

Archibald, Russell D., and Richard L. Villoria, *Network-Based Management Systems (PERT/CPM)*, (New York: John Wiley & Sons, Inc.), 1967.

The Conference Board, *New Product Development, I. Selection—Coordination—Financing*, Studies in Business Policy No. 40 (New York: National Industrial Conference Board), 1950.

———, *New Product Development, II. Research and Engineering*, Studies in Business Policy No. 57 (New York: National Industrial Conference Board), 1950.

———, *New Product Development, III. Marketing New Products*, Studies in Business Policy No. 69 (New York: National Industrial Conference Board), 1954.

———, *The Marketing Executive Looks Ahead*, Experiences in Marketing Management No. 13 (New York: National Industrial Conference Board), 1967.

———, *Organizing for New-Product Development*, Experiences in Marketing Management No. 11 (New York: National Industrial Conference Board), 1966.

Dusenbury, Warren, "CPM for New Product Introductions," *Harvard Business Review* (July/August 1967), p. 124.

Goslin, Lewis N., *The Product-Planning System* (Homewood, Illinois: Richard D. Irwin, Inc.), 1967.

Management of New Products, 4th Edition (New York: Booz, Allen & Hamilton Inc.), 1964.

Middleton, C. J., "How to Set Up a Project Organization," *Harvard Business Review* (March/April 1967), p. 75.

Miller, Robert W., *Schedule, Cost and Profit Control with PERT* (New York: McGraw-Hill Book Company), 1963.

Pessemier, Edgar A., *New Product Decisions: An Analytical Approach* (New York: McGraw-Hill Book Company), 1966.

Stilian, Gabriel, and others, *PERT: A New Management Planning and Control Technique* (New York: American Management Association), 1962.

Thompson, Stewart, *How Companies Plan*, AMA Research Study No. 54, 1964.

Wong, Yung, "Critical Path Analysis for New Product Planning," *Journal of Marketing* (October 1964), p. 53.

Index

About the Author

DAVID B. UMAN is assistant to the president of Whitehall Laboratories, Division of American Home Products Corporation. He is an engineering graduate of the University of Connecticut and has received an M.B.A. degree in management at the Graduate School of Business, City University of New York.

Mr. Uman has implemented network analysis and program management concepts in new product development and corporate development streams at Lever Brothers Company. Formerly a management consultant, he is experienced in long- and short-range planning, forecasting, production management, and operations analysis. Mr. Uman was formerly assistant to the president of the Brass Rail–World's Fair Organization where he implemented PERT to a massive development program.

Mr. Uman is a member of the American Management Association, the Society for the Advancement of Management, and the American Institute of Industrial Engineers.